CW01086263

SO YOU THINK
YOU KNOW ABOUT
FREEMASONRY?

Ray Hudson

First published in 2014 by Aziloth Books

British Library Cataloguing in Publication Data

A catalogue record for this book is available from the British Library

ISBN-13:978-1-909735-23-1

Printed and bound in Great Britain by Lightning Source UK Ltd., 6 Precedent Drive, Rooksley, Milton Keynes MK13 8PR.

MASONIC BACKGROUND

As the author of a tome entitled *So You Think You Know About Freemasonry* I should give the reader details regarding my provenance and experience that leads me to assume to write such a book.

I am an active member or have been an active member of every recognised Freemasonic order governed by the United Grand Lodge of England or governed by Mark Masons Hall, or that demands, in the very least, that you are a Master Mason under the United Grand Lodge of England. I do not belong to any Co-Masonic Order, or Freemasonic Order that does not subscribe to the principles, tenets and landmarks of the United Grand Lodge of England, whether direct or indirect.

I have taken or experienced over 250 different Masonic degrees, some current, some no longer formally practiced.

I am a practising member 3 Masonic Study Groups. One that simply discusses on a question and answer basis all aspects of Craft Ritual. Another deals entirely with Esoteric and Spiritual matters that are to be found within Masonic ritual. And the last, but perhaps most relevant, is one that has a collection of extremely old and possibly defunct rituals and ceremonies that we study, and discuss the merits contained in them.

So many things have changed within Masonic ritual, especially Craft and Chapter, that it is quite refreshing to go back to the original writings and intentions of the creators.

One lesson I have learned, and learned well, is that many words used centuries ago held a completely different meaning to what we might hold their definition to be today.

I have studied for the past 25 years every aspect of

Freemasonry visiting UGLE Library, the Library of the Rosicrucians at Hampstead, The British Library, various Masonic Museums around the country and in Scotland, and hopefully, will continue to do so for many years to come.

So I hope that you can see that I have a reasonably solid platform from which to bring to you my findings based upon all my researches and Masonic experiences.

READ AND ENJOY

Ray Hudson
March 2014

CONTENTS

INTRODUCTION

Why have I written this book? The answer to this simple question is equally simple; it is because I have been asked to do so many, many times. Going around the country lecturing to the many Lodges and Chapters that invite me, I usually get allocated 45 minutes or so in which to discuss the Craft/Chapter ritual and its meaning. The manner in which I have developed this aspect of passing on knowledge and understanding is not to read impassively from a prepared paper, allowing many to drift off into a contented "nap" until the next gavel, but to involve the Brethren in some interaction with me in exploring the various aspects of the Rituals. The Brethren would be involved in conducting a degree ceremony, so why not involve them in an interactive lecture. In this manner they ask me questions, I ask them questions, we then discuss the various answers that have become attached to many aspects of each degree, and examine the logic of each answer. The nonsensical reasons are instantly dismissed and the logical, which invariably turn out to be the right answers, are generally accepted with a great deal of surprise and astonishment. In this manner I have never done just 45 minutes. It has always been much, much longer, one even lasting 3 hours. This was not my own doing but simply that the Brethren became so involved that they did not want to finish too quickly. This solidly proved to me that the value of the information that I had acquired to pass on and the style of so doing, was the right way. It is from these activities that I have been consistently asked to publish a book with all the information that I have gathered over 26 years of solid research, in order that the enthusiastic Brother can constantly refer back to it. So, here it is.

I make no claim of originality, I am neither judge nor historian, but simply an enthusiastic Masonic researcher that patiently sifts the wheat from the chaff, and there is plenty of the latter, in order to simply bring a better understanding of the beautifully crafted Masonic Ritual. Our ancient Brethren, the compilers of our ritual, knew what they were about. Understood their aims and knew the best manner in which to procure them. A true understanding of the Masonic Ritual will reveal the full beauty of its written word, and the full power of its underlying principles and precepts.

The sources of my research are far, far too numerous to mention, and indeed would require a book on their own. I have no personal desire or wish to prove my reasoning or knowledge, but simply to put it to the reader and leave him to make up his own mind whether to use it or abuse it, as long as he goes on his way rejoicing and, in a like manner leaves me to do the same.

In the 25 or so years that I have been involved with Masonic research and history, I have learned many things. I am quite content to pass on 90% of this acquired knowledge, in fact the acquisition of knowledge is a total selfish waste if, indeed, it is not passed on. The 10% that I will not pass on is that which has become attached by some Directors of Ceremony, Secretaries, or other ill-informed Brethren who, as an explanation to a question put to them, and not wishing to show their ignorance or lack of knowledge, invent or create some romantic explanation which then gets accepted and passed on, simply because it has come from what is suspected to be an experienced Freemason. This situation appears to have occurred on numerous occasions, and I shall be demonstrating these occasions constantly throughout this book. It has also led to the well-known Masonic phrase, "Todays' mistakes are tomorrows' traditions" How very true this phrase is.

It is my wide and varied experience that this passing on of misinformation is not restricted to the lesser experienced or "light blue" Mason, but is also very well spread among what is regarded as the upper echelon or "Dark Blue and Gold's". Knowledge certainly does not come with rank, at least not in my experience. What does come with rank and the Dark Blue is appreciation for great service to the Province or Grand Lodge, in areas of general service to the Craft, and in many, many cases are very well deserved for those reasons. I once gave an interactive lecture on Craft Ritual, at the invitation of London Grand Rank Association, at Great Queen Street, where a Senior Visiting Grand Officer of 51 years within Freemasonry, so strongly doubted a correction I made to a widely accepted mispronunciation, that he made inquiries to the Grand Librarian as to the validity of my point. I was very pleased when I received the good grace of his apology accompanied by a copy of the letter he had received from the Grand Librarian informing him that I was correct. This very point will be demonstrated in detail at the appropriate place in the relative chapter.

The most common error perpetrated by so called Masonic researchers is falling into the trap of applying modern understanding to phrases and words written many centuries ago. One simply cannot apply our modern thinking when interpreting ancient manuscripts or writings. Words and sometimes actions had a very different meaning for our ancient Brethren than what it has in our terms of today. Even in our time the meanings of some words have changed with each generation. This is due to local slang, modern phraseology, even texting on a mobile phone. For example, when I was a teenager anything WICKED was, naturally deemed to be evil and nasty, whereas to today's teenagers it is held to mean the exact opposite. This is just one example, but there are many, and in Masonic terms the word WORSHIPFUL has no religious connotation whatsoever, it means respectful, as demonstrated in that other long standing and traditional system of the law, the term "YOUR WORSHIP", when talking to the Judge, who, from his learning and eminent position, commands only respect, and not religious adoration.

In writing this book I suppose that I am an accessory to my "death" as a Masonic lecturer, as in acquiring it the avid reader will have no need for personal interaction, but in reality there is nothing better than a live show, this is just the script, so with that comforting thought of an assured masonic future let me commence with this task of bringing you a daily advancement in Masonic knowledge.

The only way to keep our membership, especially the younger Freemasons, is to supply the correct answers to their questions. Comments like, "That's what it says in the book" or "that is how we have always done it" will no longer suffice. With information available at the speed of thought, the enquiring mind must be satisfied with a logically realistic answer. All of Freemasonry's tomorrows depend upon the explanations given today in order that our wonderful traditions and aims do not get lost in a sea of ignorance. I trust that in some small way this effort of mine will go towards addressing what seems to be a common problem within our fraternity. When knowledge is not passed on frustration and boredom begin to set in, and the whole objective of Freemasonry becomes pointless. This cannot be allowed to happen.

Now I must state that I do not recommend this book for Entered Apprentice's or Fellow Craft's as I would hate to spoil the wonderful ceremonies that lie ahead of them. In order to produce a book for the majority of Freemasons, one must venture into all areas of Freemasonry with an open confidence of writing within its pages, to accommodate this end I hope that Master Masons will also deter such young Freemasons as EA's and FC's from availing themselves of the information within this book, until they are regularly qualified to fully appreciate it and enjoy it.

Ray Hudson

February 2014

CHAPTER ONE

THE CRAFT

One of my personal gripes about some ritual workings is the constant references to "MASONS" and "MASONRY". Both these words, in their correct use, latterly refer to the artisan craft of Stone Masonry, and the former to the artisan craftsman himself. Whereas all rituals quote "…..but as we are not operative but Free and accepted or speculative Masons…." Why do some rituals constantly use the term Mason and not FREEMASON, and MASONRY instead of FREEMASONRY. We are in fact Freemasons practising Freemasonry, as the ritual plainly states and as such should be referred to in this way.

In order for you to understand and appreciate the evidence of my researches it makes sense to illustrate where I believe Freemasonry emanated from. In this way a better understanding should be realised regarding the rituals and ceremonies. With this aim in view, let me begin.

There being no real definitive official explanation as to the origins of Freemasonry, we must accept that many diverse opinions will be expressed as to those origins, and the wild imaginings of many fanciful and romantic writers and scholars will burden the shelves of many Masonic libraries and even the homes of the Brethren. Some of these writers are extremely skilled in the use of the English language and are able to weave a structural story that is so convincing that it is difficult for the ordinary man to deny.

It is logical that only those involved with and practising Freemasonry can objectively write about it. Those who know and understand its ceremonies, its true aims, precepts and principles are the ones most likely to write logically as their views emanate from a platform based upon actual first hand knowledge and experience, and are therefore the writers that should be taken seriously. So often the worst writing by non-masons is usually on particular matters taken completely out of context and adapted solely to confirm their preconceived wrong ideas. These less creditable "amateurs" are driven by pure speculation and hypotheses as demonstrated by current trends of fictional, romantic conspiracy theories. To fully appreciate, understand and write about archaeology, golf or running a business effectively, you must have dug the dirt, played the game to a reasonably high level, and for the latter, worked from the ground floor upwards in your chosen field. Experience will always count above speculation.

My own views rest on simple unromantic language, but, I hope, also carry a great deal of logic and evidence proving aspects present in the rituals of the Masonic degrees.

I am sure that the system and objects of FREEMASONRY to which this fairly modern title has become attached, has been in existence, in some form or other, since time immemorial, and possibly enjoyed a very similar status among certain areas of society, albeit under some other name or title such as; Magi, Priests, Philosophers, Collegiate, etc., picking up the social language and scientific understandings of the time as it progressed and developed and eventually refined into its present format.

We should not delude ourselves that we are the first society to have the privilege of what has become known as Freemasonry, including its rituals, teachings, aspirations, principles and tenets. I am personally convinced that much, much earlier civilisations had such a belief system, right from the Sumerians, into the Egyptians, into the Jews, into the Greeks, into the Romans etc. etc., albeit under a different name. Over the millennia the system has developed, matured and eventually become polished into what we now call Freemasonry. Over time all structured systems evolve and improve as knowledge and understanding improves and brings greater insight to bear on its aims and achievements. Also social changes and opinions will also effect similar changes and understandings. Freemasonry has benefitted from such effects.

Modern Masonic history claims an affinity back to the ancient Egyptians and perhaps further. The story that four Masons met in a pub and decided to form the Grand Lodge of England, and together with their mutual friend the Prince of Wales, the beginnings were formed in 1717. I do not doubt the integrity of the intentions of this Masonic morsel, but I feel that it is sadly lacking in meat and marrow. So to supply the meat and marrow I did a great deal of research and now present my own views as to the origins of Freemasonry.

I first wrote a paper, so called, "Freemasonry..... whence did it take its rise?" many years ago, and being constantly aware of the many new findings in archaeology, also attentive to the other sciences that analyse ancient cultures and the like, and appreciating that research by its very name defines that, that which is searched is now re-searched, and is a never ending study, I still have found nothing to change the view I held when I first wrote the paper, in fact I have found more to sustain my original views.

As you may have already experienced, the arguments that proliferate this question are many and varied, and have been discussed in numerous volumes by countless notable scholars. Each bringing something fresh and of value in their work, but somehow failing to connect all the links in one study. I hope, in my small way, to redress this situation, or at least to provide you all with a few more links to your existing chain.

Of all the discussions and opinions regarding the origins of Freemasonry, there are three that are dominant over the rest:

1). That it rose from the operative skills, and over the centuries gradually became speculative, due to the diminishing need for operative skills, as technology and construction evolved.

2). That it emanated from the Guilds and Liveries within the City of London.

3). That it was brought from the East to the West through the auspices of the Knights Templar.

Looking intently at the first argument, there are many, many good reasons for taking this view. Naturally our ritual leans heavily towards this science. We call ourselves MASONS. We speculate on many aspects of this skill, and make many allusions to this special craft. Many respected researchers fall into this trap, which, by its very content, is easy to do. But I hope to prove that Freemasonry did not evolve directly from this admirable craft, but was itself grafted on to it to disguise its originality, for very poignant reasons.

Think of yourself, for the moment, as a medieval apprentice mason, serving a seven year apprentice under a proven skilled Master Mason. During this period, you eat, sleep and dream every aspect of this skilled operative craft. Learning and practising every skill and art involved in Masonry. Demonstrating in stages the different skills you have learned. At the end of this very arduous and intense training period, you are expected to present to your master a piece of commissioned work involving all the different skills acquired over this seven year period. This was called your "Masters-Piece" or masterpiece. If your piece passed the very strict standards of craftsmanship expected, you were accepted as a Master Craftsman, and could go out into the world and make your mark. You would either set yourself up on your own, or more likely travel to one the many large building projects going on at that time, and there were many, Churches, cathedrals and castles being built all over the country. Having arrived at one of these intended structures, and received employment, your ability and skill would be discovered by the quality of your work, and no other way. If you lied at the interview by professing to be better than you actually were, this would be immediately shown up by your lack of actual skill in the finished product. For as an apprentice you would not be shown or instructed in a higher skill until you had fully mastered the previous one. As these structures took anything from five to a hundred years to complete, any cowan or impostor would soon be discovered. The point I am trying to make is that there was no need for any passwords or penalties, as there was nothing to protect in the operative skills, you had either mastered them or you had not, and the standard of your work would have been the governing factor and not your knowledge of certain passwords or handshakes. There may well have been a sort of hierarchy or fraternal comradeship among the operative masons themselves that may have required a password, but surely would not have merited a severe penalty of death in some form. It was the standard of your work that decided your employment and scale of wages. If, as generally accepted, the Master Masons secret word commanded your employment, then the employee, which in those times was generally an ecclesiastic or clergyman, would have to know the secret word of a Master Craftsman. This makes no sense and belies the importance stressed on the secrecy of the actual word. As a modern example, in the Craft, if a Fellowcraft had knowledge of the Master Masons word, and tried to pass himself as a Master Mason, it would not be too long before the genuine Master Masons became suspicious of his lack of knowledge of the ritual and rubric of the Third Degree. Once discovered he would be quickly dismissed. The same must have applied to the ancient operatives. Although the Freemasonic system utilises many aspects of this artisan craft of Masonry to illustrate its many aspirations, and I can understand how so many writers are "lured" into this attractive aspect, none the less I feel that it is simply what it claims to be ; "allegorical" and "veiled". So, as romantic as the thought may seem, and as romantic as some masonic writers and observers try to make it, it does not seem logical to me for the need for passwords or the importantly stressed penalties. I was, and still am, convinced that there was a very much more serious importance applied to these aspects of the modern Craft. Therefore, for these reasons, I dismiss the possibility of these origins.

Men have a natural tendency and inclination to "team up". As modern Freemasons have a word and a handshake that binds them, so do military regiments, schools, guilds and other male groups, have a motto, and an heraldic symbol and objective to distinguish their collective individuality and separateness. This system is nothing new. Because Freemasons keep the signs and symbols "secret" this has led the romantic writers and novelists to speculate on the most incredible conspiracy theories.

Giving similar intense study to the second argument,

I find there are too many historic and chronological differences for this point of view to have lasting merit. Although the Guild system is of ancient lineage, and is of a very similar physical structure, and holds many of our moral aspirations with similar respect, I cannot accept that Freemasonry rose from these fine institutions. The Guilds were formed as a sort of protection for the members and as some sort of recourse for the customer. They were able to control quality and price, much the same as some Trade Federations do today. The Guilds also supervised the apprenticeships, which included a moral aspect towards oneself and the community. Also the guilds laid a very heavy stress on religious aspects, especially Christianity, as did the Operative trades, something the Craft has studiously avoided since its supposed inception, and there is a very sound reason for this avoidance. Like the operatives there was no serious reason for the guilds to instigate passwords or even penalties, like those relating to the Craft. Having been awarded the Freedom of the City of London myself, in 1974, it is my belief that the Guilds borrowed some-what from the structure of Freemasonry.

What astounds me in respect to the Operative Masons and the Guilds is their heavy concentration on the religion dominant at the time which was Christianity. If Freemasonry takes its heritage from the operative stone masons or the guilds surely our rituals would reflect that leaning and depict Christian buildings and Christian stories and events, of which there are a multitude, to name just a few, Stonehenge, York Minster, Canterbury Cathedral, The Tower of London, etc.etc. But no, Freemasonry is all about Judaism and Jewish history, how odd is that? Throughout the millenia any belief system or stream of variable thought that appeared to threaten or was contrary to that of the powerfully established religion of the day namely the Roman Catholic Church, incurred the equally powerful retribution and persecution of that religion, and history meticulously records such retribution on collectives as well as individuals, so much so that I need not dilate on such events here. Hence the secrecy under which some variable thinkers operated. Over the centuries many Popes have banned their Catholic followers from joining Freemasonry, to the point of ex-communication. Why was this if Freemasonry emanated innocently from the operative craft of Stone Masonry or even from the Guilds? No, there must be a more sinister reason for such a total ban and constant issue of Papal Bulls prohibiting membership. No Papal Bull has ever been issued regarding the Craft of Stone Masonry or the Guilds, only that of Freemasonry. So for all the reasons stated, I have to dismiss this possibility with the same enthusiasm as I did the first.

So finally we arrive at the third possibility, which obviously must be the origin that I favour. That Freemasonry took its rise from the Knights Templar has, after many years of study and research, become positive for me for many many historical reasons, which I shall now relate to you. But first, for those of you not so familiar with the Knights Templar and its history, I will first give a thumbnail picture of their rise to power and influence, and fall from grace. I will stick to the actual recorded historic facts, omitting the legends and myths such as the Holy Grail and Ark of the Covenant.

In the year 1099, nine Knights from Gaul, led by Godfrey de Bouillon entered Jerusalem, and befriended King Baldwin I, who was an uncle of one of the nine, to convince him to allow them to reside in the Temple grounds. Allow me to digress a little at this point and throw into this pot of speculation and hypothhesis a tit bit of history concerning these nine Knights before they sojourned to the Holy Land. It was necessary for them to meet often if only to plan their journey, and for the lack of any Preceptory or nominated meeting place, they met in each others houses. So much so that they became known, by the local populace as "House brothers", which in the Gallic of the time was "FRÈRE MAISON". Personally I do not see such a great leap of faith necessary to go from Frère Maison to Freemason. I have often wondered why Freemason is expressed as one word and not two. If there is such an insistence on Freemasonry emanating from the Operatives, why not use the term Free Mason instead of Speculative. Anyway enough of this particular digression, let me go back to my discourse on the Knights Templar. There is archaeological proof, and academic writings, that these knights tunnelled underneath the centre of the temple and possibly up into the level just below the Sanctum Sanctorum or Holy of Holies. They must have discovered something, and there are many legends speculating on what actually was found, because subsequently Hugh de Payens petitioned Baldwin II for permission for these nine knights to establish themselves as a new religious order. This permission was granted. They took the name "The Poor Fellow Soldiers of Christ and the Temple of Jerusalem". They became known by many titles, but were popularly remembered as Knights Templar. For the next nine years little is recorded of their actions. Neither did they take in any new recruits, rather strange for a new order. All these nine knights came from Champagne in Gaul, and most were closely related in some way. Through Bernard of Clairvaux, nephew to one of the nine and Abbott of the Cistercian Order, and later to be canonised as St.Bernard, they obtained a Rule from the Pope. With the powerful religious backing of the Pope and therefore the Holy Roman Catholic Church, plus

Bernard of Clairvaux, known as the "Second Pope", and King Baldwin II of Jerusalem, they were now officially formed and recognised as such.They were not originally set up as an Order of Chivalry, but primarily as an escort of protection for the pilgrims making their way to the Holy Land. Whereas the Hospitallers or Knights of St.John had been formed to administer aid and succour to those pilgrims who fell foul to the many bandits on their route.

Bernard championed their cause vociferously and urged that they be supported with gifts of land and money and encouraged aristocratic young men to forget their sinful lives and take up the sword and the cross as Templar Knights. So successful was his canvassing that the King of France gave both monies and substantial grants of land, which was promptly followed by similar gestures from the nobility. King Stephen of England did likewise. The knights were granted many productive manors which provided a continuous income.

So, Hugh de Payens had left Jerusalem as one of a small group of an obscure unofficial order, returning just two years later with 300 knights, the backing of the Pope and many of the kings of Europe, and untold wealth and land. What was it exactly that they could now command such attraction and support that they could not in the beginning? Was it what they discovered from their tunnelling? Remember that the most powerful organisation at that time was the Holy Roman Catholic Church, and for them to throw their great weight and support behind this group of nine Knights there must have been a powerful reason. Many researchers, far more academic than I, have speculated on what these nine Knights actually discovered, that I need not dilate on it here. Whatever they originally discovered in their tunnelling, or whatever knowledge they learned from their sojourn in the Middle East, it led them to become secretive. What they knew or had learned must have been different from the belief system of their backers, the all-powerful Roman Catholic Church, otherwise why the need for such secrecy? The more powerful and influential they became, the more secretive they became, as they obviously had much more to protect.

Over the next 200 years they were to become the most powerful and respected force in the then known world. They built preceptories and castles all over Europe and the Middle East. They were great builders responsible for tremendous cathedrals and churches, many of which still stand today. They also built up a tremendous fleet of ships, and conducted trade with spices and silks etc. Their fighting prowess was justifiably legendary. They were also skilled in commerce, law and financial matters, holding the treasuries of both England and France. The banking system is attributed to the Knights Templar. Many European kings were in their financial debt, especially King Phillip of France. They were considered experts in law and helped to structure the legal system of England at the time. Their main preceptory, and the surrounding area, in London, is still steeped in the legal profession.

At their zenith of power and wealth, as is always the case, envy became the bed for malicious rumour. Their secret rites, initiations and ceremonies were speculated to be heretical and blasphemous. Phillip, King of France saw this as an opportunity to grab their wealth and power, and therefore automatically absolve himself of his huge financial debt to them, he conspired with the Pope, whom history proves was in actual fact his puppet, to decimate the Order on charges of heresy. To all of which the Pope agreed. This was effected in absolute secrecy, so that on Friday the 13th October 1307, 5,000 Knights Templar were arrested and imprisoned in France. This date (Friday the

13th) has held fear and dread for many people ever since although the origins have become lost in the mists of time. When the arresting soldiers went to take charge of their fleet of ships in La Rochelle, it had gone, together with the Templar treasury, so the secrecy could not have been as absolute as was believed. The Pope insisted that the regents of the other European countries should activate his ruling in the same way. But most at first refused, finding the accusations unbelievable of such a revered order. This delay gave the overseas based knights the time to regroup and make plans for their escape accordingly. The arrested knights, in France, were subjected to the most excruciating torture, and many falsely confessed, under these conditions, to the charges of heresy, and were subsequently burned. Many died faithful to the principals of the Order. Even the Grand Master, Jacques de Molay, confessed under torture, but recanted his confession, along with the Treasurer of the Order, before meeting their death from burning. This whole process from arrest until the death of the Grand Master took nearly seven years, and there are many authoritative books available on this subject, giving great detail of all the events. The other main countries handled this situation very differently. In Portugal the Knights Templar disbanded and joined The Knights of Christ, and continued under that banner. In Germany they joined up with the Teutonic Knights, some even joined the Knights Hospitaller of St. John, or as they became known The Knights of Malta, who are the inspiration behind our own St.Johns Ambulance Brigade, who have as their insignia the 8 pointed cross of the ancient Order.

It is believed by some academics, and I also see good reason for this, that some knights crossed the Alps and entered some of the principalities there, eventually forming many into one solid unit and becoming the country we know as Switzerland. If you consider the ethos of Knights Templar, their penchant for secrect codes, their development of the banking system, their neutrality etc., it is not too far removed from the manner and respect that Switzerland is held in internationally. Finally on this point, it is accepted that one of the early codes of the Knights Templar was mirror-imaging or the reversing of things to the eye. If you look at the banner and tunic of the Knights Templar and then look at the national flag of Switzerland you will see precisely what I mean. Now to continue.

The Pope then gave a decree that the Knights Templar were formally disbanded and declared that all their wealth and land acquisitions be handed over to the Knights Hospitaller, after having taken some for the Holy See as administrative costs, likewise the King of France. The Knights Hospitaller, rather than standing by their brother knights, eagerly grabbed this opportunity of swelling their own ranks, wealth and power. A fact that the fugitive Knights Templar never forgot. As I have mentioned before there are many authoritative books on this subject each with their own theories and explanations, some very far-fetched and some more realistic.

The Knights Templar over the period of their open existence, fast developed into an organisation of many diverse skills. Warfare, Farming, Husbandry, Banking, and Building. The experts demonstrating this last skill were known as "The Children of Solomon" and were so accomplished that the buildings still exist today demonstrating the quality and craftsmanship that still amaze the experts. It is obvious that this was a separate unit within the Knights Templar, just as the naval fleet were a separate unit. There were many distinct separate units that specialised in different skills, and the one that became the most notorious was the fighting unit, or the actual Knights. The Children of Solomon were so appreciated by the clergy of the time that they were absolved of any involvement of the heresies the actual Knights Templar were accused of and were subsequently allowed to go free and continue in their great and glorious work. It would come as no surprise to me to learn that many of the persecuted Knights subsequently claimed only attachment to the Children of Solomon in order to maintain their survival and were taken in because of overall loyalty and thereby able to maintain their traditions under the guise of the building fraternity.

You must appreciate that the religion dominant at this time, the Holy Roman Catholic Church, was all-powerful, superior in power even to many European Kings. And totally used this power in any way they saw fit to procure the subjectivity of its global congregation, and to further strengthen its own hold and power. Anyone who spoke out against the workings of the "Church" was duly deemed a heretic and put to the stake. Therefore people were genuinely in fear of their lives, and having witnessed, over a few short years, the total obliteration of a once omnipotent knightly order, felt total justification for their fear and dread.

I said "totally obliterated", but was it actually ?

We must now look at what could have happened to those knights that appear to have fled !!

First we must look at the Fleet of the Knights Templar and the treasure, whatever that was. As I mentioned earlier they must have had prior knowledge of their impending doom for they were nowhere to be found. The main fleet containing the treasure found its way to Scotland. A country with its own problems, being ex-communicated as a country, by the Church of Rome, therefore the Papal Bull was never sent there, and consequently was non-effective, thereby making it an ideal haven for the fleeing fugitives. There was also strife within itself over its sovereignty, and it was constantly at loggerheads with England. One of the prominent senior family groups of the Knights Templar through its inception and progression was the original Gallic noble family called St.Clair. This family formed a stronghold in Scotland and became the Sinclairs, who throughout the centuries have held prominence with Scottish nobility and higher government, even to this very day, being very well recorded in Scottish history and many recent books on the Chapel at Rosslyn, which was built by the Sinclairs, and is believed to hold a very strong Masonic/Templar influence.

Some of the fleet continued to sail the seven seas preying on the ships of the very Catholic countries they felt were responsible for their demise. These ships were manned by "pirates and corsairs", a phrase I would ask you to bear in mind, and sailed under the banner of the "Skull and Crossbones", a very strong emblem of the Knights Templar which is to be found on many Templar graves, especially in Scotland, as it was the way many of them were buried. These emblems of mortality are extremely significant in our Freemasonry.

It is said in many academic quarters that a small fleet of ships sailed the seas in search of Catholic ships in order to prey on them and take their gold etc., and as these pirate ships appeared to have no designated country of origin and therefore could fly no national flag, they sailed under the only flag they knew which bore an emblem familiar to them which was the Skull and Crossbones. One enthusiatic Knight who dedicated his life to this seeking of revenge was one Roger de Montfort and it seems that it is from him that the term "Jolly Roger" was appended to the the flag displaying the emblems of mortality. It is supposed that the booty collected was some sort of recompense for the booty taken from the Knights Templar. Hence we have the origins of piracy. I cannot confirm any facts supporting this hypothesis but it does hold as much a resonance of possibility as it holds of romance, so I leave it to you, the reader, to decide for yourself.

Bearing in mind the delay on the part of the English King to implement the Papal Bull against the Knights Templar, this would have afforded the persecuted knights time to re-group and receive the news that their fleet and many of their brothers in arms had found a safe haven in Scotland. They would have needed to travel there under cover, which of course was no real problem for they were quite used to developing passwords, codes and all the necessary subterfuge for fugitives on the run. It is somewhat strange how words originally designed for a "cloak and dagger" purpose become absorbed into modern vocabulary without many realising its true origin. One of these words is "ROSE" as in the ceiling rose, through which we hang our central light, why not a tulip or dandelion, why a "ROSE", I will digress and explain. Not used specifically by the Knights Templar, but probably in some aspect or other. There was an old system called in Latin "SUB-ROSA" meaning "under the rose" The ancient Romans used to hang roses, particularly white roses over their dining tables to signify that anything said under the roses was deemed safe and never to be quoted outside. In the Middle Ages houses used to surround their doorways with white roses to signify that this was a sympathetic household or a "safe house. The Victorians would make plaster emblems of roses and stick them in the centre of their ceilings over the dining table to signify confidence and freedom in after dinner conversation. With the advent of gas and electricity being placed in the centre of the room, the pipework or wire was passed through the middle of "The Rose", and the name has continued ever since although many do not realise its origins, age or significance.

This type of sign would have been second nature to their particular system of secrecy, which had been finely honed over the past 200 years. They developed a system of "safe houses" and collaborators throughout England leading, by various routes up to Scotland. Where they were welcomed for their various skills and possibly most of all for their undoubtable fighting skills, and battle expertise, as the conflagrations between Scotland and England were now coming to a head.

We should now look at the Battle of Bannockburn and Robert the Bruce. Legend has it that Bruce herded all the elderly folk, women and children to drape white sheets over their heads and at the strategically given signal, to come charging and screaming over the hill and hopefully scare the English Army into retreat. According to romantic legend this is what happened, and did put the whole English Army to flight! Romantic ? Yes., Realistic ? No ! The more likely scenario is that after agreeing certain terms with Robert the Bruce on a victory at Bannockburn, the fugitive Knights Templar agreed to advise and assist him in his plight, being heavily outnumbered by the English Army. Agreement was obviously reached for at the most strategic moment of the battle the Knights Templar led a fearsome decisive charge towards the ranks of the English Army. The sight of such a fearsome force in their white mantles together with their famous battle-cry "Beau Seant", meaning "be noble", or "be glorious", charging full pelt on their famous war horses, with their fearsome reputation going before them is what put the fear of God into the

English Army. And they did indeed flee, pursued by the jubilant Scots, who immediately slew all they caught.

This incident is the main reason for the success of the Scots at Bannockburn, plus, of course, the strategic planning and logistics of the battle skillfully devised by the Knights Templar It is historically recorded that at Bannockburn, immediately after the victory Robert the Bruce founded the first Lodge of Kilwinning, and I quote, ".....for the reception of those Knights Templar who had fled from France...." This obviously was part of the Templar deal with him.

Many scholarly historians have attributed the rise of Freemasonry in this manner.

In those days of fanatical religious persecution where there were dire consequences for anyone who hinted at the possibility of being even slightly heretic, the need for anyone fully accused of such a crime, whether true or false, to flee and go underground, was paramount, if you wanted to survive. And the Templars wanted to survive in some form or another.

As the Knights Templar were predominantly, to all intents and purposes, a fighting force for Christianity, throughout their formidable history, they also had a "building arm" known as "The Children of Solomon" who were entirely steeped in the building of many, many marvelous cathedrals, castles and churches, the construction of which still amaze the architects of today, and this influence plus their own chivalric culture, together with that which they became embroiled over the centuries, would naturally be influenced by any ascetic knowledge they may acquire from the many cultures and schisms they encountered on their many travels, particularly in the Middle East. As I have mentioned earlier, to escape persecution and to preserve their beliefs many Knights disclaimed their knighthood and claimed affinity to the Children of Solomon. The most sensible candidate for an expression of their precepts would have to be one that they were already very familiar with, and that candidate was the art of building, or MASONRY. Like a river which begins at the top of a mountain, pure and unsullied, and, on its travels to its final destination, becomes infiltrated many times, sometimes enhanced and sometimes polluted, or even changed off its course, but inevitably its journey must cause change, however slight, from its pure beginnings. Templarism cannot be excluded from this analogy. For example, the religious persecution brought about the biggest change to Templarism, whilst it was on its metaphoric journey. It forced its change to MASONRY. As, up until that time, Templarism had built as a shield to its possible actualities, the outward image of "Warrior Monks", and I personally have no doubt that this was in reality just a shield for whatever their real purpose might have been, for there is no record of them having actually protected pilgrims on the road to the Holy Land, which if you remember was their original supposed "raison d'etre". So the Templars were quite used to this sort of subterfuge, and to slide into another "shield" more suitable to the times than warrior monks, would have been relatively simple for them, and to me quite obvious. Thus, in 1314 ended this official historic order known as the Knights Templar. Incidentally "The Children of Solomon" were not incuded in the persecution of the Templars and were allowed to go free, but they would naturally be invested with the culture that dominated their artisan profession. Maintaining a secret system under the guise of the artisan profession of these "Children of Solomon" would have been relatively simple. Just a thought.

In addition to the absolving of the Children of Solomon

of any heretical acts, it seems so were the actual Knights Templar, but the latters absolvement was suppressed possibly on the instructions of the Philip the Fair, as this extract printed below confirms.

The Chinon Parchment is a historical document discovered in September, 2001, by Barbara Frale, an Italian paleographer at the Vatican Secret Archives. On the basis of the Parchment, she has claimed that, in 1308, Pope Clement V absolved the last Grand Master, Jacques de Molay, and the rest of the leadership of the Knights Templar from charges brought against them by the Medieval Inquisition. The Parchment is dated August 17-20, 1308, at Chinon, France, and was written by Bérenger Fredoli, Etienne de Suisy and Landolfo Brancacci, Cardinals who were of Saints Nereus and Achileus, St. Cyriac in Thermis and Sant'Angelo in Pescheria respectively. The Vatican keeps an authentic copy with reference number Archivum Arcis Armarium D 218.

Another interesting historical fact is that during the Albigensian Crusades, which was a murderous purge by the Roman Catholic Church on the Carolingians simply because they held Jesus Christ to have been a mortal man, not a God but a great prophet, many Knights Templar protected many senior Carolingians by affording them "safe houses", even on occasion lodging them in their own properties. Why would the Templars safeguard the individuals that held this Gnostic view of Jesus Christ? Did they secretly hold similar views formed from the greater knowledge they learned from their time in the Middle East? If they did they would certainly have to keep them strictly secret as the power of the Roman Catholic Church, as history records, was powerful and relentless in its persecution of so called heretics.

This ends the thumbnail history of the Knights

Templar, and now would be a good time to bring in some of the Templar "icons" to be found in Freemasonry today.

Looking back at the charges of heresy made against the Knights Templar, one of the most serious was that they "trampled on the cross of Christ". The reality of the actual step that they took was exactly the same action made by us in the step that we take. To them it represented the actual " T " bar cross now accepted by most biblical scholars to be the actual style of the true cross of Jesus, and not the artistic traditional style with the extended upright. This step was taken by the Knights in reverence and solemnity and in sacred memory of the crucifixion. But how simple it would be to accuse exactly the opposite, much the same as the innocence of our ceremonies has been interpreted as devil worship by some imaginative writers. When translated to Masonic symbolism this step represents the " Tau " cross, said to be the most perfect figure in geometry, and represented on the Installed Masters Apron, indicating that three steps have been completed, and also has importance in other degrees in Freemasonry. We must remember that in transferring from Templarism to Masonry, they also, in the process, de-Christianised most of their symbolism, something they had to do in those fanatically Catholic dominated times. This simple transfer of symbolic representation loses nothing of its importance or impact. Most of the symbolic penalties of Freemasonry represent to "those with eyes to see", the sort of tortures that their comrades were subjected to, during the persecution. One of the extreme penalties suffered by those that refused to submit to the charges of heresy, was that of being hanged until almost dead, the gut being slightly opened, and the entrails pulled out and burned while the victim was forced to watch. When finally dead from being "Hung and Drawn", the body was cut into four pieces and put on spikes to be displayed in the four corners of the city as a warning to others. Thus "Hung, Drawn and Quartered", It doesn't take a lot of imagination to see the hidden similarities of the 3rd degree, the four corners of the city being represented by the four Cardinal Winds of Heaven. The Templar Initiation ceremony and progression was similarly effected by degrees, as the aspirant progressed, more was revealed, after a test of merit. When one studies the romantic and symbolic writings of those times it is not too difficult to align the story of the demise of the Templar Grand Master Jaques de Molay with that of Hiram Abiff. Jaques de Molay, when captured and tortured "confessed" to all the accusations levied against the Templars, but on his being burned at the stake he withdrew his "confession" and established the firm principles of the Order as being untarnished and pure. So euphamistically in the romantic language of the time one can say that spiritually he perished under brutal torture but rose to his former honourable state on his being burned at the stake. The one thing that finally clinched it for me was the names of some of the "Officers", and the one that takes the prize is the name of the officer who stood outside the door of their preceptory, being armed with a drawn sword, and was called in old Gallic, "Le Tailleur" (pron. Tye-er).Meaning, "He who cuts". Nowhere else have I seen a more sensible origin for this very important office, and believe me there have been many suggested, but this one has logic, history and a positive connection to support it, rather than the romantic speculation that dominates the other interpretations of this Lodge Officer.

It has been hinted by many eminent historians that there was an organising force behind the Peasants Revolt. Even Winston Churchill in his History of the English speaking people, mentions the significance of a Great

Society behind it. It does seem incredible to me that an insignificant illiterate peasant can rise from nowhere, and for eight weeks command, control and organise up to a 100,000 peasants to form an incredible rebellion. The logistics involved in doing this today would be quite phenomenal, but in those days with no phone, fax, or any communication other than personal contact, it would appear nigh on impossible, certainly beyond the capabilities of a mere peasant. It is now realised that the majority of the buildings that the peasants destroyed were the churches and residences of the Knights Hospitaller. The Templar properties were left intact. How were the peasants able to make this distinction!! The two most important people that they beheaded in their apparent anarchy, were the Archbishop of Canterbury, head of the Roman Catholic Church in England, and the Grand Master of the Knights Hospitaller. Why were these two so special to the peasants? Could it be that in exchange for assistance, organisation, and a system of secret codes, from the fugitive Knights Templar, a promise of revenge was carried out by the two leaders of the revolt, the most significant one being called Walter the "Tyler", just where do you think he got his title from ?

The word Cowan is very interesting and was first introduced in Old Scottish Masonry to describe a person who could do the work of a stonemason but did not possess the Masons Word, and has often been used by masonic writers to prove the link to the Guilds, as this word is used by the guilds to describe an unqualified craftsman, or non Guild member trying to practice the craft. But I am afraid they are wrong. A careful perusal of the "Old Charges" reveals the qualifications for acceptance into a Masonic Lodge. The applicant must be free born of a free mother, without physical impediment, sane, and not in his nonage or dotage, that is to say not too young or too old. For if you think about it, how could you, under the religious persecution ruling at that time, being a fugitive, fully trust someone who was not quite all there, through their lack of common sense, or being crippled in some way, or through being too young or too old. the latter two being covered by the words nonage and dotage. In old Gallic there is a word "COUENNE" (pron. KOO-WAHN), which means "ignoramus" or "bumpkin", aptly describing just the sort of person to whom you would be most unwise to trust your secrets, least of all possibly your very life. It makes profound sense, if you are a group of fugitives, on the run from religious persecution, to have an armed guard outside your door to keep off idiots and snoopers.

Staying with this Scottish connection there is a famous poem by the Scottish poet Robbie Burns which relates a story about a crofter and his dog. Most crofters dogs were black and white. Burns refers to the dog with the phrase "..........his bawsant face", which means his black and white face. The Templars battle flag was black and white and was called the Beauseant. It does not take a great leap of faith to go from the Gallic Beauseant to the Highland Bawsant. Robbie Burns was a famous Freemason, exactly who got what from whom?

In one of the degrees of modern Freemasonry the aspirant is informed that this degree will make him a Brother to "Pirates and Corsairs", I ask you, what does a pirate or a corsair have to do with a stonemason, it can only refer to the fate of some of the fleeing Knights Templar, and to be a constant reminder of those that took to the high seas to escape the persecution.

The toast to Absent Brethren is self explanatory.

The toast to "poor and distressed freemasons where're dispersed over the face of earth and water", can only refer to the scattered Knights Templar, and, in the hope that the religious persecutions end...."wishing them a safe return to their native land, should they so desire"...fairly self-explanatory.!!!!!

The Knights Templar used to wear white lambskin "drawers" under their mantles as a sign of purity, and try as I did I could find no evidence of the operative masons wearing white lambskin aprons, they wore aprons made from rough cloth or ordinary cowhide but not white lambskin. Also I could find no actual evidence of ancient stonemasons wearing white gloves. But according to ancient manuscripts the Knights Templar wore white gloves to preserve their hands for when they "touched God". Lastly, the obvious fact that the ceremonies revolve around their first and main objective The Temple of Solomon. To crown this explanation of the origins of Freemasonry, there is a very popular order in Freemasonry that does confirm that Freemasonry did emanate from the Knights Templar, but does not quote any of the reasons of proof that I have offered here, it just simply states it as a fact.

Bearing in mind, and if you accept the facts previously given, the Knights Templar now having achieved some sort of revenge for their terrible persecution, and possibly avenged the death of their own Grand Master, Jacques de Molay, they were now able to carry on their pursuits, albeit under an apparently different guise, and to quietly watch the developments evolving, and therefore pick the appropriate time for revelation, as and when they saw fit.

Having brought us from 1099 to about 1385, you may well ask "Why did they wait until 1717 to come out of the closet, another 330 years?" A good question, which I will briefly answer. You must bear in mind that England was still a very staunch Catholic country, influenced strongly by the Roman Catholic Church, so it was extreme folly and potentially life threatening to reveal any other religious beliefs, no matter how tenuous.

But soon the wheels of change would slowly begin to move, as I will now explain with a brief overview of the events leading up to 1717.

Most of the 15th Century passed with little historic change. According to ancient manuscripts "Masonry" was steadily growing, and attracted many great thinkers of the times.

On 22/8/1485 King Richard III lost the throne and his life at the Battle of Bosworth to Henry Tudor, the Welsh Earl of Richmond, who married Elizabeth of York. His eldest son Arthur died in 1502 from T.B. The next son Henry, aged 18, succeeded in 1509, as Henry the VIII, and married the widow Catharine of Aragon within 6 weeks. After many failed births, in 1516 a daughter, Mary, was finally born. Henry then married Anne Boleyn and sired Elizabeth. Henry was very belligerent and self centred, and caused many rifts and arguments with the Roman Catholic Church and its staunch followers. He did not take kindly to being directed by someone from abroad who was not even a King. So he then formed the Anglican Catholic Church, amid great unrest and general civic dissension against the Roman Catholic Church, due once again to their stern rules and continuing acquisition of wealth, power and especially land.

Edward VI was crowned in 1547 aged 10, ruling for 6 years, and under the guidance of his advisers , repealed the laws of heresy and thereby opened the doors for Protestantism.

Lady Jane Grey, backed by a Non-Catholic group, took the throne over Mary, who was a staunch Catholic, and ruled for nine days. Mary then ousted her and ruled for five years, as a fierce Catholic, being ferocious in her faith and its implementation, ordering 300 executions in 3 years. This ferocious campaign increased the religious bitterness already prevalent among her subjects. She went down in history as "Bloody Mary".

Elizabeth, when queen, re-instated her fathers Anti-Church laws and was ultimately ex-communicated by the Pope. Under Elizabeth England moved more towards Protestantism, some going even further and creating "Puritanism".

1603 saw the death of Elizabeth. The country was in such religious turmoil, which ultimately led to civil war. There were many assassination plots. The most famous attempt by Guy Fawkes. We still celebrate this failed attempt on November the 5th, but few people today realise that the effigy burned on the fire was originally that of the Pope and not as it is supposed today, of Guy Fawkes. Such was the level of anti-Catholic feeling at that time.

James I greatest achievement was the King James Bible, which is still the biggest selling book today. This was achieved through his close friend and mentor William Schaw, who is the same individual responsible for the Schaw manuscripts or statutes, famous in Freemasonry, and from which most of our rituals emanate. James died in 1625 and was succeeded by Charles I. Throughout his reign religious unrest increased even further, until in 1642 Civil War broke out with Charles and the Church on one side and The House of Commons with Oliver Cromwell on the other. It is interesting to note, at this juncture, that there are many quoted incidents regarding the "Freemasons" of both sides, the most distinctive being, that although a Puritanist, Cromwell was also a Freemason, and when his army entered Scotland to rout the Catholics and High Anglican Church followers, although they burned and sacked Rosslyn Manor, they did not touch the famous

Chapel in any way shape or form. They razed the manor to the ground but left Rosslyn Chapel unscathed. Something totally out of character for their religious beliefs but obviously not their stronger Masonic ones.

Charles was defeated in 1642 and on January 30th 1649 he was beheaded.

Cromwell as Protector was too puritanical and dictatorial and died in September 1658, his son was too ineffective and the Army invited Charles II to take the throne. On 29th May 1660 Charles came home. In 1666 the Great Fire of London occurred.

The existence of Freemasonry is well documented during Charles II reign and during James II it grew even more, but James was a Catholic. The "Protestant leaders" invited Mary and William of Orange, both strong Protestants, to take the throne.

In 1701 a law was passed allowing only members of the Church of England, namely Protestants, to take the throne, thereby precluding any future Catholic monarch. This law is still in force today. Also in 1701, Anne, daughter of James II, and the last of the Stuarts, being a staunch Protestant, became Queen.

In 1707 the Union between Scotland and England joined their two crowns and "Great Britain" was born.

In 1714 Anne died and George I began the Hanoverian Dynasty. The country was ruled by Government and strictly Protestant.

In 1715 the Jacobite rebellion surfaced and was quickly put down.

There have, over the centuries, been many accusations that Freemasonry has been quietly instrumental in instigating changes in governmental law and statutes, changes in social reform etc. etc. Even have they been hinted at being the power behind the throne. Noting the comments of Churchill, mentioned earlier regarding the Peasants' Revolt, and the apparent influence of the advisers and also the influences in other areas such as the Non-Catholic group, Protestant leaders etc. The relationship of William Schaw and King James. The same for the Templars and eventually the Sinclairs and Scotland. The final Union of Scotland and England. We must also bear in mind that one of the main and possibly most laudable of Freemasonrys' principles is to bring about, by the most peaceful means of democracy and understanding, a better world for all. It is difficult not to draw the obvious conclusions.

So ended the centuries long failed struggle to return England to Catholicism and the Holy Roman Church.

With the power of the Roman Catholic Church and its dominant Catholicism removed, now it was safe for the "Knights Templar" to come out of hiding. As Scotland, being ex-communicated, was attractive to the fugitive Knights Templar, so England, with the death of dominant Catholicism, was now attractive to the Knights Templars' new image of "FREEMASONRY" !!!

Two years later, in 1717, 4 Masonic Lodges decided to "come out of the closet", now that they had no further need for secrecy, and no reason to hide from the establishment.

For me the facts speak for themselves, both historically and chronologically.

Now I would again like to digress a little, but still stay with the connection of the Knights Templar.

History records, and I have seen no academic or historian speculate from this point, that the Knights Templar were fiercely Christian, at least at the outset of their pursuits. They became backed by the most powerful Christian authority of the time, commanded Christian pilgrims as followers and supporters. These facts are undoubtedly true, proven and recorded. This being so it begs a great question. Why is the main Masonic Orders of the Craft and the Holy Royal Arch, Jewish? Why are the mainstream Orders in Freemasonry generally depicting some biblical event from the Old Testament, an incident in Jewish history or culture. The Knights Templar were a Christian group, backed by the most powerful religious Christian group in the western world, which possibly still remains so, the Christian Roman Catholic Church. The Mother Grand Lodge of Freemasonry is acknowledged to be the United Grand Lodge of England, which being based in London, abides under a social and legal system that reflects Christian Protestant ideals and teachings.

I can only deduce that the Knights Templar discovered something, or came into some powerful knowledge that led them to form perhaps differing religious beliefs, which were contrary to what the all-powerful church, which were also their backers, was preaching and would have believed by all, that they had to maintain the image of their original intention and religious structure, or risk termination. This secret change obviously eventually leaked out and hence history records in detail the outcome. I have often asked why, when this acknowledged mother country of Freemasonry, whose laws and culture are predominantly Christian, whose reigning monarchs not only have to be Christian but must be Protestant, whose history records having twice evicted the Jews from its shores, and whose history records much antagonism against the over powerful domination of Catholicism, finalising in its suppression, has itself such marvelous religious buildings to commemorate, and such tremendous events in its religious development, we, that is Freemasonry, commemorate predominantly Jewish buildings and events. Personally I have no problem with that whatsoever, as the principles of Judaism are in reality the basic principles of Christianity, and therefore the basic principles of the laws of this country. I digressed here to simply further strengthen my hypothesis that modern Freemasonry emanated from The Knights Templar.

Had it emanated from the operatives, that is the actual stonemasons, or the guilds of this country, then I truly believe that we would be celebrating, Stonehenge, York Minster, Canterbury Cathedral, the Tower of London, or some other great structural achievement, of which there are many examples, but we are not. We are celebrating, specifically, Jewish religious history and culture. There has to be a profound reason for that, and I hope that I have sufficiently demonstrated that reason to be the Knights Templar.

Before proceeding I would like to provide some detail on that enigmatic character mentioned earlier, albeit briefly, and that is William Schaw, author of the Schaw Statutes. He is little appreciated or even known by many Freemasons, but played such an integral and important part in the formation and structure of early Freemasonry that still echoes prominently within modern Freemasonry, that should not be forgotten or ignored. I will give the quote from Oddvar Olsen's marvelous book, "The Templar Papers", which is a collection of papers by eminent academics on the Knights Templar. This quote is from the paper by Robert Lomas entitled "The Early History of Freemasonry"

"WILLIAM SCHAW, the great architect of the Craft"

William Schaw was born around 1550 in Clackmannon, near Stirling. His father, John Schaw of Broich, had been keeper of the king's wine cellar. By the age of 10 years, William was employed at court as a page to Mary of Guise (we know this because the Queen Dowager's accounts recorded his name on the list of her retainers for whom mourning was purchased). That same year his father was charged with murdering the servant of another Laird.

William next appeared in Scottish records when he signed the "Negative Confession," a document that James VI and his courtiers had to swear by in order to assure the Reformed Church that the king and his retinue were not trying to bring back the Catholic Faith. (William was a Catholic, but seems to have been flexible enough in his religious attitudes to stay out of trouble with the Kirk. As Stevenson comments: "Like a number of other Scots in court circles, though remaining a Catholic he avoided actions that might provoke persecution, probably attending Protestant services from time to time."

Schaw became James VI's Master of Works towards the end of 1583. About a month after his appointment, the king sent him on diplomatic missions to France (on the basis of his diplomatic, as well as building skills). This seems to be confirmed by the fact that the king chose Schaw to help entertain the ambassadors of the king of Denmark, who came to negotiate the restoration of Orkney and Shetland to Denmark.

Schaw must have got on well with the Danes, because in 1589 James sent him back to Denmark to escort his new bride, Anne of Denmark, to Scotland. Schaw went on to become Queen Anne's Chamberlain, and a great favourite of hers. As his monument recalls:

Queen Anne ordered a monument to be set up to the Memory of a most admirable and most upright man lest The recollection of his high character, which deserves to be Honoured for all time, should fade as his body crumbles Into dust.

It was in 1590 that Schaw began to take an interest in Masons and their organisation. The first written evidence of this is a letter composed under the authority of the king's Privy Seal, and addressed to Patrick Copland of Udoch (near Aberdeen) confirming his right to act as"wardanie over the maister masons of Aberdene, Banff, and Kincarne". Stevenson believes that Schaw may have been considering reorganising the mason craft under a number of regional wardens, and therefore used the historical precedent of the Coplands of Udoch to reestablish the principal of regional wardens. However, eight years after confirming the authority of a regional warden in Aberdeenshire by privy seal, Schaw took on himself the role of a general warden of the Craft in Scotland. The post was a new one that Schaw created, and it met with the approval of a number of unamed "maister maissounis," who attended a meeting on the Feast of St. john (in Edinburgh) in 1598.

Schaw, who was the king's Master of Works, acted as agent for the throne in all state building works. This gave him a great deal of control over the Masons of Scotland, and so he was only rationalising a state of a ffairs that was already in existance. His first Statutes contained 22 clauses.

The first clause insists that all Masons "observe and keep all the good ordinances set down before, concerning the privileges of their Craft set down by their predecessors of good memory and that they be true to one another and live charitably together as becomes sworn brethren and companions of the Craft." Here Schaw is referring to a system of regulations still known to Masons as the Ancient Charges.

The remaining clauses deal with how the lodges shall be ruled and governed, and how the work of the masons should be managed. There are two particularly interesting items. One contains the first health and safety directive ever issued within the building trade. It says: "That all masiteris, in charge of works, be very careful to see their scaffolds and ladders are surely set and placed, to the effect that through their negligence and sloth no hurt or harm come to any persons that works at the said work, under pain of discharging them hereafter from working as masiteris having charge of any work, but they shall be subject all the rest of their days to work under or with another principle masiter having charge of the work." Stern discipline indeed, for any Master Mason who did not take care that his workers were properly secured when they worked in the dizzy heights of a great cathedral or a Scottish grand house. Today's factory inspectorate would not quarrel with the intentions and sanctions of this 16th century Masonic legislation.

The other interesting item concerns how the Master of the Lodge shall be chosen: "That there be a warden chosen and elected each year to have the charge over every lodge...to the effect that the General Warden may send such directions to that elected warden as required."

The Master of the Lodge (Warden) has to be lected each year, and Schaw, as General Warden of the Craft intended to issue any instructions via the elected officers of the Lodge to the Masons. This was a highly democratic system he put in place (some 50 years before the Civil War got around to addressing the same questions of democratic accountability in England).

All in all, this was a far-sighted and fair document, and it has the obvious intention of simplifying the general management of Masons in Scotland. It takes account of the ancient traditions of the order and respects existing rituals, makes proper provision for safe working practices, and providdes for regular democratic feedback from the "Maisteris" of the Lodge. It was issued with the endorsement of all the Master Masons who had attended the feast of

St. John meeting in Edinburgh in 1598, as the closing sentences show "and for fulfilling and observing of these ordinances, set down as said here, the group of maisteris here assembled this day binds and obliges themselves hereto to be faithful. And therefore has requested the said General Warden to sign them with his own hand, to the effect that an authentic copy hereof may be sent to every particular lodge within this realm."

This document is also the first time that any lodge has been instructed to keep written records of its proceedings. (The oldest lodge minutes in existence are those of Edinburgh St. Mary's Chapel, which started immediately after this meeting with Schaw.)

The first Schaw statute tells us a lot about early Freemasonry. It demonstrates that our antient Scottish brethren met in lodges, that these lodges were ruled by Masters or Wardens, that there was a system of meetings at a higher level than the lodge, that the lodges were obliged to keep written records of their activities, and that they were bound to observe the ancient ordinances of their craft. All of these aspects have survived within modern Freemasonry, and this is the earliest written evidence of their introduction.

Schaw formalised the present-day system of Masonic Lodges. A lodge is not just the building where Masons meet-it is also the body of men who make up that group. It has its own traditions, heirarchy and records to prove what it has decided-but it is basically a democratic unit inherited from a time when democracy was not yet supposed to have been invented.

However there is more to this story, because a well established lodge existed out on the west coast of Scotland. This lodge, known today as Mother Kilwinning, was not based in Edinburgh, but rather on the coast of Ayr, on the grounds of Kilwinning Abbey. The wardens of Mother Kilwinning Lodge were accustomed to issuing charters to other groups of masons-so that these groups could form themselves into new lodges-and they claimed rights over the Mason Craft in Ayrshire.

Schaw's first Statute did not recognise the rule that Kilwinning claimed in the newly-created Masonic rating. The following year, 1599, on the Feast of St. John, Schaw issued his secong Statute, this time from Holyrood House (one of the King's palaces). They confirmed the statements in the first Statute, but went on to assign formal status to Kilwinning Lodge.

When Schaw had held his first formal meeting as General Warden of the Craft, again on the Feast day of St. John the Evangelist, Kilwinning Lodge sent Brother Archebald Barclay to present a case that it should have a role in the new way of ruling the Craft. Varclay was successful in making his case, as Schaw went on to confirm that Kilwinning should be allowed to maintain its ancient practise of electing its officers on the eve of the winter solstice. It was also assigned the rank of "second lurge of Scotland," and its wardens were to have the right to be present at the election of all other Wardens of Lodges within Lanarkshire, Glasgow, Ayr and Carrick. A Warden of Kilwinning was to have the power to summon and judge all wardens of lodges within this area, with power delegated by Schaw as General Warden of the Craft. The Wardens of Kilwinning were to conduct regular tests of the Masons within their jurisdiction to ensure they were properly trained in "the art and craft of science and of memory."

With this clarification of the most important of the ancient ordinances and the adjustment to the pecking order between St. Mary's Chapel and Kilwinning, Schaw apparently had settled Freemasonry into a more stable structure. However, he had even greater ambitions for his fledgling new organisation. Schaw wanted the king to become Grand Master of the Order, and he wanted a Royal Charter to confirm this status on the Craft forever.

He had one problem. The Masons would not accept a cowan as their Grand Master. Even though he was a king, if James was to become the Grand Master Mason, he would first have to become a Mason.

In 1584, Schaw had assisted his close friend Alexander Seton (later Earl of Dunfermline, and a member of Aberdeen Lodge) in designing a house for Lord Somerville. The master masom employed to carry out the work was John Mylne. In 1601 Mylne was Master of the Lodge of Scoon and Perth. This Lodge was situated in Scoon, (modern spelling, Scone) which is the ancient place of the coronation of the Kings of Scotland. (The Kings of Scots have traditionally been crowned at Moot Hill, within the grounds of the Palace of Scoon. So, Scoon was a fitting place for a king to be made a Mason.)

On the wall of the Lodge of Scoon and Perth hangs a painting of a very important Masonic event (the initiation of King James VI). The official entry of the Lodge on the Roll of the Grand Lodge of Scotland simply says the lodge existed before 1658. This date refers to the charter of the Lodge, and is a set of rules that explain how the lodge was governed. The document is signed by the Right Worshipful Master (J. Roch), and two wardens (Mr. Measone and Mr. Norie). This same Charter records the event depicted on the wall of the lodge room. The Charter states: "In the reigne of his Majesty King James the sixth, of blessed Memorie, who, by the said John John Mylne was by the king's own desire entered Freeman, meason and Fellow-Craft. During his lifetime he mantayned the same as ane member of the Lodge of Scoon, so that this lodge is the most famous lodge within the kingdom."

As I have mentioned, the Mylne family figure a great deal in the early history of Freemasonry-no less than 3 generations of them (all with the Christian name of John) held the Mastership of the Lodge of Scoon and Perth between the late 1500's and 1658, when the Scoon Charter says the mastership passed to James Roch. This James Roch was the signatory to the document that records the making of James VI as a Freemason in 1601.

The second John Mylne (son of the John who initiated King James) had carved a statue of the king in Edinburgh in 1616. In 1631, this Mylne was appointed Master Mason to Charles I, and in 1636 resigned the office in favour of his eldest son, also named John Mylne (all the Mylnes seemed to call their eldest son John), who had been made a Fellow Craft of the Lodge of Edinburgh in 1633. This third John Mylne took part in the Masonic meeting in Newcastle in 1641, where Sir Robert Moray was made a Mason (Moray is the first person documented as having been made on English soil.)

So the grandson of the man who initiated James VI went on to initiate Moray. There is every reason to believe that Moray received a family account of the initiation of James VI, and may have been well aware of the close links between the Stuart kings and Freemasonry before he became involved with them. Moray went on to found the Royal Society which is still one of the most important scientific societies in the world today.

But the real question that needs to be asked is how James VI, King of Scots, came to be made a member of a lodge of Freemasons.

The political purpose of the king being made a Mason should now be clear. To complete his designs for the Craft,

Schaw needed the King to be a Mason. James VI loved ritual, masques and dressing up. From all accounts he would have delighted in the initiation ceremony. Schaw now had every thing he needed in place to propose a Royal Grand Master Mason for the Craft, to be followed with the issue of the Royal Charter that confirmed his authority as Lord General Warden of the Craft. However the Mason of Scotland had different ideas.

When Schaw had created his second statute, he had been on the verge of obtaining a Royal sanction for the privileges of the Craft. However, at this point it appears he was forced into backtracking. A poerful group of Masons insisted that he issue a document, now known as the first St. Clair Charter. Of this document, Stevenson writes:

(It) *can be seen as indicating...that Schaw was forced to change his plans (for obtaining a Royal Charter) to take account of the claims of the Craft...which were too strong for him to resist. Schaw's death in 1602 and the move of the king to England on the union of the Crowns the following year may have disrupted attempts to win the king's support.*

Now that Schaw had confirmed the claims of Kilwinning in its role as a minor Grand Lodge, the other lodges had recognised that Schaw could be put under pressure, and could be made to adjust his ideas. Obtaining the agreement of the Lodge of Scoon and Perth to initiate King James VI seemed to have been Schaw's first move towards uniting the Lodges of Scotland under the Grand Mastership of the King. (There is a Masonic Order which automatically makes the reigning King of Scots its Grand Master, known as the Royal Order of Scotland). The consequence of James's making the Lodge of Scoon and Perth his mother Lodge would, as the minutes say, be "so that this Lodge is the most famous Lodge within the kingdom."

This move would undermine all the jockeying for position which had gone on earlier. Edinburgh had already been named as first lodge, Kilwinning was officially number two, and Stirling was positioned third in seniority. But now as the Royal Grand Master's Lodge, Scoon and Perth was poised to take precedence over all other lodges. By initiating the king, the Lodge of Scoon and Perth was outflanking all of their brother Masons.

Schaw was now put under pressure by the Lodges in the east of Scotland (Edinburgh, St. Andrews, Haddington, Acheison, Haven and Dunfermline) to acknowledge another ancient authority in Freemasonry, that of William St. Clair of Roslin. As Stevenson comments: "Though in William Sinclair the masons has found a gentleman of ancient lineage willing to be their patron, theyhad not found a respectable or influential one...If the masons had had a free choice in seeking a suitable patron to advance the craft's interests they would never had chosen the laird of Roslin!".

William St. Clair, third and last St. Clair Earl of Orkney, and the builder of Rosslyn Chapel (where the oldest evidence of Masonic ritual is carved into the wall) had been the second most powerful man in Scotland until 1471, when he had been forced to split up his holdings. The Baronies of Roslin and Pentland had been transferred to one of his son's (Oliver, Lord Sinclair). From Oliver they then passed first to another William, and then to an Edward, before vesting in the particular William Sinclair we are concerned with.

This William Sinclair was a Catholic who kept falling foul of the Kirk. He used Rosslyn Chapel to have one of his children baptised in 1589. (Rosslyn was not a Parish church, but William was unperturbed by the outcry this caused.) The minister who conducted the service, however, was forced to make a public plea of forgiveness. A year later, the presbytery of Dalkeith accused Sinclair of "keiping images and uther monuments of idolatrie" in Rosslyn.

The Kirk officials had to postpone interviewing him, however, as he had been arrested and charged with threatening the king's person. When he was freed, the Kirk pursued him, insisting that Rosslyn should not be used as a place of worship and insisting that William force his tenants to attend the parish Kirk. They also suggested he set an example and become an elder of the Kirk. William declined, saying he was "insufficient" for the position. He proved his point soon afterward, when he was forced to make a public confession of fornication with a local barmaid.

To add insult to injury, he told the Kirk he could not remember if all of his bastards had been baptised. When he was ordered to do public penance for his acts of fornication (by sitting on the repentance stool), he refused unless he was supplied with a quart of good wine to help him pass the time.

If one was to judge from the number of summonses issued to Sinclair to keep the peace and to refrain from attacking individuals, it would seem that he was fond of both wenching and brawling.

Hay, the historian of the Sinclair family, described him as " a lewd man, who kept a millar's daughter for the purpose of fornication." He eventually ran away to Ireland with his mistress, abandoning his wife, his son William (there are a lot of William Sinclairs in this story!), and the Craft of Scotland.

This, then, was the man the Masons of Scotland preferred to have as their Patron, rather than let the Lodge of Scoon and Perth take precedence over them. William the

Wastrel, as the Laird of Roslin was then known, had his power as the last St. Clair Earl of Orkney behind his claim, and he was the keeper of the most important Freemasonic shrine in Scotland, Rosslyn Chapel. His patronage was the only way to thwart the ambitions of the Mtlne family (which Schaw had unleashed, via the Lodge of Scoon and Perth). The claim of the Laird of Roslin could be supported by appealing to the first sentence of the first Schaw staute; "...that they observe and keep all the good ordinances set down before concerning the privileges of their craft by their predecessors of good memory."

The first St. Clair Charter takes just this line when it says:

"Be it known to all man that the Deacons, Maisters and Freeman of the Masons with the realm of Scotland with the express consent and assent of William Schaw, Maister of Work to our Sovereign Lord do assert that from age to age it has been observed amonst us that the Lairds of Roslin has ever been Patrons and Protectors of use and our privileges like as our predecessors has obeyed and acknowledged tham as Patrns and Protectors."

So it would seem that Schaw's attempt to obtain a Royal Charter for the Freemasons failed because some Lodges insisted on adhering to an older tradition (which linked them to the Sinclairs of Roslin). The outrageous character of the man they gave their loyalty to suugests that the tradition must have been important to them. Otherwise they could have gone along with Schaw' plan and taken James VI as their Royal Patron. Certainly, the king's joining of the Craft had encouraged many of his courtiers to also join the Masons. Among them Lord Alexander, Lord Hamilton, and David Ramsey (Clockmaker to the king and gentleman of the Privy Chamber) who joined the Lodge of Edinburgh.

When James moved to London he continued to take part in ceremonies that involved acting out the role of King Solomon (the role taken by the Master of the Lodge during the opening and closing ceremonies). {I take a different view of this comment, as detailed earlier. RWH} And he certainly does not seem to have been secretive about it. Sir John Harrington, who spent an evening at James VI's court while he was entertaining King Christian of Denmark in 1617, reports: "After dinner the ladies and gentlemen of the Court enacted the Queen of Sheba coming to King Solomon's Temple. The lady who took the part of the Queen of Sheba was, however, too drunk to keep her balance on the steps and fell over onto King Christian's lap, covering him with wine, cream, jelly, beverages, cakes, spices, and other good matters that she was carrying in her hands."

This was not the only occasion James was reported to have carried out dramas connected with Solomon's Temple. James, however, became so obsessed with reenacting the story of the events surrounding Solomon's Temple that his courtiers dubbed him the Vritish Solomon. But he also carried out regular Freemasonic ceremonies. As William Preston reports: "In 1607, the foundation stone of this elegant structure [part of the Palace of Whitehall] was laid by King James, and his Wardens who were attended by many brothers, clothed in form. The ceremony was conducted with the greatest pomp and splendour."

So, prior to his coming to England, James VI, through his Master of Works, William Schaw, developed the modern lodge system of Freemasonry in Scotland. By the time James had been initiated into Freemasonry at the Lodge of Scoon and Perth in 1601, he had become fascinated with the rituals of Solomon's Temple (which form an important part of the basis of Freemasonry). James had made Speculative Freemasonry fashionable in his court in

Scotland, and then brought the rituals of Freemasonry to England."

Hopefully now one can see and appreciate the connections of William Schaw, Scotland, the Sinclairs and therefore the Knights Templar, the cohesion of which must draw one positively to the logical conclusion that I trust I have amply illustrated.

Having done that, I can now begin to give complete explantion and detail as to the 3 rituals of the Masonic degrees known collectively as The Craft, which will fit precisely with this hypothesis I have just delivered above.

CHAPTER TWO

THE OPENING OF THE LODGE

IN PREPARATION FOR WORK.

Before any Lodge can conduct a ceremony or, indeed, do any work whatsoever, it must be "opened" or prepared for such work. This opening is usually conducted by the three principal officers, namely the Worshipful Master, the Senior and Junior Wardens. No Lodge can be fully open and prepared for work unless it is "JUST, PERFECT AND REGULAR". This is a much used phrase, which, I have discovered on inquiry, that few Freemasons fully understand or appreciate. When is a Lodge JUST? I have often asked this question and have been given many spurious answers which are, in turn, guesses. Again the real reason is simple and uncomplicated logic. In reality there is nothing really complicated in Freemasonry, only the individuals that make up the Brotherhood. Now a Lodge is JUST when the Volume of the Sacred Law is open and the three great lights are in position. When is it PERFECT? When there are seven or more Brethren present. When is it REGULAR? When the Warrant is present and displayed.

The Lodge is opened and prepared for work in a set traditional manner with each Officers' duties explained, so that all present are fully aware of who is doing what. Then after this standard ceremony the Worshipful Master declares the Lodge "duly open for the purposes of Freemasonry........." . He then gives the knocks of the degree, to alert his two Wardens. The Senior Warden responds by similarly giving the degree knocks to alert the Brethren seated in the North and West, while the Junior Warden will accordingly respond in the South to alert the Brethren seated in the South and East. Now here we have a conundrum. Invariably I have witnessed that the Worshipful Master will knock, the Senior Warden will knock, and then immediately the Junior Warden will knock and the Inner Guard will jump to his feet to inform the Tyler, by giving the knocks on the door, that the Lodge is ready for work and ready to receive latecomers. Whilst in reality, the Lodge is not ready, as the three Great Lights are not yet in position. How many times I have heard the Tylers responding knocks, and the IPM has not even got off his chair to set the three great lights in position. I have often asked the Junior Warden "Why did you knock on the opening of the Lodge?" and invariably the reply I get is "because he did" (pointing to the Senior Warden).

As I mentioned earlier there are several different workings of the Masonic rituals currently in operation, each with only subtle differences, such as an odd word or two or a slight difference in a perambulation or part of the rubric. Generally the essence of the ritual is the same, and in this ritual the actual duties of the Junior Warden are most specifically detailed, but appear to be either forgotten or not understood by many.

When an Initiate is taking his first degree a most important part of the ceremony is when the Worshipful Master draws his attention to what is known as the Three Great Lights. He explains their position and importance and that no Lodge can be ready for any work unless those very important three Great Lights are in their respective positions. Then, in the future, when a Junior Warden is appointed and invested, an important part of the ritual explaining the duties of the Junior Warden is given by the Worshipful Master to the Junior Warden, which goes along the lines of......" particularly that part of your duty which relates to the admission of visitors, lest by your neglect any unqualified person should gain admission to our assemblies, and the Brethren be thereby led to a violation of their obligations....." So here is a strict instruction not to let the Tyler know we are ready to receive visitors until the three Great Lights are actually in position. This means that whenever the Worshipful Master knocks, which is followed by the Senior Wardens knocks, the Junior Warden does NOT knock until the IPM has opened or adjusted the three Great Lights, then and only then is the Lodge ready for work and ready to receive visitors or late-comers and is therefore the correct time for the Junior Warden to instruct the Inner Guard by giving the knocks of the degree, to let the Tyler know accordingly. This the Inner Guard does by giving the knocks of the degree, on the door of the Lodge. The Lodge being properly prepared for work in the first degree, it may now commence. Similarly the closing should be regarded in a like manner, that is, when the VSL is closed and the Square and Compasses are likewise adjusted, it is only then that the Junior Warden knocks and subsequently the words that follow "....and it is closed accordingly." Suddenly have a sense and logic in time with the action taking place.

THE FIRST DEGREE IN FREEMASONRY OR ENTERED APPRENTICE.

Freemasonry is made up of Degrees and Orders. A degree is a ceremony that contains a secret sign, a secret grip (known as a token) and a secret word. An Order is a group of degrees that illustrate a particular theme or event in biblical Jewish history. It is not my intention to reveal any of the traditional secrets of Freemasonry, I have no intention of spoiling any future ceremony that an aspiring candidate might enjoy. This determines that I must, at times, speak in an inferred manner rather than a fully revealing one. My simple intention is to explain aspects of the Craft ceremonies in such a way that the reader may enjoy greater the ceremony he has experienced, and, hopefully, may be inspired to make some researches of his own.

A candidate for Freemasonry is known as the Initiate, simply because he is Initiated into the Craft. Having given certain proofs of his religious and social beliefs and his character, he is invited to a Masonic Lodge room or Temple as it is known, to be Initiated or to take his First Degree. It is interesting that it is known as a Temple and not a Church, Cathedral or Ministry. I do not know of any Christian house of worship that is known as a Temple. Does this term stem from Judaic biblical history or from the Knights Templar, or perhaps both, I will let you decide this small point.

Having arrived for the ceremony he is introduced to the Brethren of the Lodge in an informal and friendly manner. He is not told anything about the ceremony he is to experience, and that is but right. The whole ceremony is meant to impress upon him the high importance of Freemasonry and its principles, aim and precepts.

Before he is prepared for the ceremony, the Lodge is prepared by being "opened" in the First degree. With the Lodge Officers and Brethren in their respective places the Worshipful Master "opens" the Lodge in accordance with the ritual of the particular workings that the Lodge operates under. As far as I can determine there are 52 different "workings" currently being operated in the United Kingdom at this time. Mostly the difference is the name of the actual working and maybe a few different words and instructions in the rubric, but mostly they all follow the same Solomonic Legend or Old Testament story of the building of King Solomons Temple.

The basis for the story is that the Jewish God Jehovah gave instructions originally to Moses to build the Ark of the Covenant also a Tabernacle to house the Ark. With the progression of Jewish history as depicted in the Old Testament it finally fell to David, King of Israel to build the first actual stone Temple in Jerusalem. But as David's sword was "so stained with blood" he was not actually permitted to do this, so he instructed his son Solomon to supervise the building of the structure to a plan detailed in the scriptures. The legendary wisdom of Solomon prevailed, and he enlisted assistance from some of the greatest artisans in the then known world, and so the Temple was built and completed in just over 7 years. The degrees of the Craft detail the different stages of construction and particular events that occurred during this 7 years plus of building this magnificent structure.

As in most ancient writings and legends, there is more than one way of interpreting the written word. There is the obvious level of "what you see is what you get", which most Freemasons are fully content with, and there is nothing wrong in that single acceptance. Then, as the story is taken directly from the Bible, there is the religious level, which, if a Freemason wishes to see that reference and adopts it as an aid to his faith, then, equally, there is no problem there either. And as the Christian Faith, the Jewish Faith and the Muslim Faith of Islam all follow the same biblical stories, as they are all actually Abrahamic Faiths, therefore the reason why this wide appeal and involvement is so universal, can be greater appreciated. Obviously there is also the historic interest for anyone keenly interested in a wider explanation of the Old Testament stories than the Churches convey, and finally there is the ESOTERIC (secret, hidden) or spiritual interpretation of those same stories. So really within the Masonic ceremonies there is something for everyone depending on your preference. The reader may benefit from a fuller explanation of the word and description ESOTERIC. This word means secret or hidden and its opposite is EXOTERIC, which defines as being open or revealed. ESOTERIC is an unusual word for a common aspect, or an aspect that is more common than appreciated. The EXOTERIC aspect of Masonic rituals within the Order of the Craft relates the building of King Solomons Temple, and plainly appears to celebrate that event. The ESOTERIC aspect alludes the building of this Temple to the building of the character of a man, stone by stone and metaphorically wall by wall, until you have raised a superstructure perfect in its parts and honourable to the builder, i.e yourself. There are many Freemasons who adopt this esoteric approach and explore and develop it for the improvement of themselves. Many believe that this esoteric approach is the actual real object and true benefits of Freemasonry, a point of view I would give no argument to. Now let us get back to our Initiate.

The first "MASONIC" person that the initiate meets is the guard outside the Lodge Temple who is known as the TYLER. I, like many other Freemasons, have been given many reasons as to this title of office, but as with any other aspect of Freemasonry, there can only be one real truth. There are many romantic explanations for this unusual office title, such as, "Oh its to do with the Tiling of a roof", this I dismiss as in the very early days, centuries ago, meetings were held, according to old manuscripts, "where the dog does not bark and the cock does not crow", which rules out towns, cities and even rural inhabited areas. There is Masonic evidence that meetings were held in the woods or copses, where the Master had 2 Assistants and a TYLER, but obviously no roof. So that romanticism about tiling a roof has to be dismissed. Similarly there are some equally dismissed explanations which are based soley on romanticism leaving the only explanation as to the origins of this title that contains history, logic and a positive connection to be the one I gave earlier regarding the Knights Templar.

The Tyler then prepares the Initiate for his ceremony. He removes all monies and other metallic substances that might be construed as having some value. In the old days this even went to removing the buckles on their shoes and any brass buttons etc. etc. So that each Initiate is in a total state of being "poor and penniless". This is done for a very special reason which will become obvious later. In some Lodges the Initiate is told to remove his shirt and trousers and is dressed in a white sort of overall. His right arm is made bare as is his left knee, and his left breast is exposed. A running noose, which is called a Cable-tow is placed around his neck and he is blindfolded (hoodwinked). In other Lodges he maintains his trousers (with the left trouser leg rolled up) and shirt (with the right arm made bare and his left breast exposed) so is prepared in exactly the same manner as described immediately above. Finally his right shoe is removed and his right heel is exposed by rolling his sock down to the middle of his foot. This is masonically referred to as being slipshod. There are good reasons for this preparation and I will give my explanations as to this preparation, starting at the top.

The Blindfold

The human being has 5 senses, each acutely sensitive. If one is removed then the other four become more sensitive. This is regularly demonstrated in piano tuners, many of whom are blind. With their sight removed their hearing becomes more sensitive and discerning. So for the Initiate having the blindfold on, he becomes more aurally aware. This heightened awareness increases the power and impact of the drama unfolding. In this way it is hoped that the words delivered and the impact of their meaning has the right impression on the Initiate, bringing the force of the ceremony completely home to him. Also it is possible that if at any time he wishes to stop the ceremony and leave the Temple, that is, prior to the completion of his Obligation, he can, and he would not have seen anything of the events taking place within the Temple. In a romantic manner it is said, in relation to his exposed left breast, that "the heart can conceive before the eyes perceive". So apart from the romantic way, there are excellent sensible reasons for the Initiate to be Blindfolded or Hoodwinked.

The Cabletow or Running Noose

This is a symbolic demonstration which, in reality, has never been effected but does add a great sense of drama for the Initiate. It is meant to prevent an Initiate from turning round and running from the door of the Temple, or even from within the Temple itself. It also has, in my opinion, another powerful impact, and that is that it represents and reminds us of the fate of many of those ancient Knights Templar who lost their lives in this manner in the terrible persecutions of 1307.

The left breast laid bare

The majority of Freemasons believe that this is done to prove the masculinity of the Initiate, and it could well be part of the fact, as the Freemasons did not and do not admit women to their ranks. I also think that there are two other equally valid reasons, and one is that the heart can conceive before the eyes perceive, and the other is to accommodate a more positive response to the poignard, a small slim sharp dagger, when it is applied to the Initiates naked left breast. Here the Initiate is asked "Do you feel anything?" The reason for this action is that if the Initiate attempted to rush forward, he would impel himself on the poignard. This of course has never happened and is, these days, more symbolic than actual, but it all adds to the drama and effect of the experience. Also later in the ceremony another sharp point is so presented to his naked left breast.

The right arm made bare

This is a simple but most important part of the Initiates preparation and is done for a very specific purpose. At a particular part of the ceremony the Initiate takes a solemn Obligation, or swears an oath to maintain secrecy and certain other promises. This Obligation is a most serious part of the ceremony and of his becoming a Freemason. This Obligation is taken in a specific kneeling position and with his right bare hand resting on the Holy Bible or the religious book of his particular choice. This situation gives an added seriousness and solemnity to the Obligation that he makes. All obligations within Freemasonry are made with the bare hand on the Holy Book, and although Freemasons wear white gloves, they are removed when the individual takes an Obligation. The reason for this is quite simple and logical. You will recall my earlier comments regarding the fact that most Masonic ceremonies depict some incident of Jewish history or culture, then it makes sense that the Holy book be open at the respective chapter that relates the particular incident that the ceremony depicts, and the bare hand shows the very important fact that there is nothing between the Initiate, or the hand, and the word of God. This action is also demonstrated in a court of law. If a witness is about to give evidence, and takes the Holy Book to "swear to tell the truth, the whole truth and nothing but the truth, so help me God," then if he is wearing gloves, the hand that is holding the Holy Book must have the glove removed. This simple but specific action demonstrates the importance and simplicity of another part of this impressive preparation.

The rolled up trouser leg

This simple, but to outside appearances, stupid part of the preparation, has been, and still is the cause of many a joke and cartoon, jibing on what is felt to be the ridiculousness of grown men walking around with their trouser leg rolled up within a Masonic ceremony. Well, as we all know, it does happen, but similarly to the bare right arm, there is a perfectly simple and logical reason for this apparent silly part of the preparation.

I mentioned earlier that in the olden times, centuries before, meetings were held in the woods or copses, and Obligations were taken in a kneeling position, as they still are today. The Initiate must kneel on the bare knee so that there is nothing between him and God's earth. Exactly matching with the bare right arm touching God's word. In the first degree it is the left knee bare, in the second degree it is the right knee bare, and in the third degree it is both knees bare. If you think about the solemnity and religious intent of the Obligation you can see that the apparent stupid preparation has a perfectly logical, and in fact serious intention that there be nothing between the Initiate's hand and the word of God, and nothing between the Initiate's knee and God's earth. This explanation completely follows through all three degrees with logic and is in keeping with the solemnity and seriousness that must be maintained when one is taking such a serious Obligation.

During the many years of my visiting Lodges and lecturing on the Craft rituals, I have been given many other reasons for the rolled up trouser leg. Most Freemasons seem to forget that when the ritual was originally created there were no trouser legs as such, simply britches and hose, so that this part of the preparation had a simplicity that was obvious. Over the centuries with the change of clothing fashion this act has been made to look more ridiculous than it actually deserves, and has attached to itself many very spurious explanations as to its reason for being. I will give just the most popular three:

1) It is to show that you are a free man and that you are without fetters or chains.
2) It is to show that you are not concealing a weapon.
3) It is to show that you are not a woman.

Apart from the fact that these false reasons totally undermine the work and ability of the Tyler, who has, on behalf of the Lodge, and on the instructions of the Worshipful Master, prepared the Initiate by removing all monies and metallic substances which must include any weapons or fetters, who then places him squarely in front of the Inner Guard for him to inspect, who in turn confirms to the Worshipful Master, and therefore the whole Lodge, that the Initiate is "properly prepared". They make a nonsense in so far as the Initiate, and the work of the Tyler, and the eyes of the Inner Guard, were not believed or trusted respectively, and totally belies the ritual, as he is prepared in a much similar fashion for the 2nd and 3rd degrees. So if he is not believed in the first degree, then he was not believed in the second and with both knees bare in the third degree, most certainly was not believed. No these other reasons have to be dismissed and the logic and importance that I have explained regarding the closeness of the Initiate to God's earth, which is now represented by the kneeling stool, is upheld.

Being slipshod

Having the heel exposed, in the manner previously given, is a simple token of humility. The tradition of removing a shoe can be seen in many cultures in the Middle East. In the Bible, when Boaz went to Ruth's father to request her hand in marriage, he took off his shoe as a sign of serious intent, and as a humbling factor. More recently when Saddam Hussein was deposed and his statue was pulled down many of the local residents began slapping it with their left shoe. Even more recently at a speech given by President Bush, he was assailed by a shoe thrown by an Arab in the audience, So the significance of the symbolism of the shoe and its removal is amply illustrated. Furthermore, and it is a distinct possibility, that the Lodge room represents King Solomon's Temple, and the ground on which you are walking is therefore symbolically consecrated or Holy Ground, and I will explain this further at the appropriate place in this book.

Having explained the preparation of an Initiate, we can now go on and explain certain aspects of the first degree.

Obviously I am not going to fully explain or detail the whole of the Entered Apprentice degree, just the salient points that I have witnessed persistently misunderstood or mis-applied.

The first point I would like to address is the position of the right hand when placed on the Volume of the Sacred Law during the Obligation. It should be placed flat with the palm downwards and the thumb placed in the form of a square. In some ritual workings, when the Entered Apprentice sign is made, the right hand is first extended in front of the body with the hand in the exact position as it was arranged when taking the Obligation. This action is to remind the mason of the solemnity of his Obligation, which in turn demonstrates that he is "a man of honour", and therefore fits in perfectly with the verbal ritual. Other workings just bring the hand straight up, not demonstrating this first position, therefore, apparently missing this important symbolic gesture.

After he has taken his Obligation and been informed of the importance of the Three Great Lights the newly obligated Brother is wheeled to the right hand side of the Worshipful Master, where he is informed of many situations that he has so far experienced. Then the Worshipful Master instructs the Candidate to "take a short step with your left foot, and place ...." Once this is done he then says, "That my Brother is the first regular step in Freemasonry.........." By using the word regular in such an emphatic way implies that there are irregular steps. And there are. The word irregular means not of uniform length, size or shape. And the irregular steps taken are those that the Initiate takes on his approach to the pedestal, each one of an irregular length.

Then the Sign, Grip and Word are given and explained and the candidate is perambulated around the Lodge and presented to the Junior and Senior Wardens in order for him to supply the proofs of his being made a Freemason. The Senior Warden is then instructed to invest him with his Entered Apprentice Apron, which he does. This investiture seriously acclaims the value of the Freemason's Apron, and claims it to be more honourable than the Star, Garter or any other order in existance. I personally feel that the claims are correct and the Apron should be afforded the pomp and ceremony that the ritual affords it by being carried on a cushion from the East to the West and presented to the Senior Warden for him to invest the Candidate with. Unfortunately some Lodges simply pull the Apron from out of the Senior Wardens pedestal and then invest the Candidate. This completely belies the wonderful ritual that accompanies this investiture. The Worshipful Master then explains further the attributes of the Apron and the manner in which it should be respected.

The Entered Apprentice Apron is of a simple nature. Plain white, symbolising purity, with a flap which, in some workings is raised up to symbolise one of the four basic elements of life namely fire, but in most workings this raising of the flap is not effected, which is a bit unusual as with most aprons designed for artisan work there was always a raised flap or "bib". The flap being in an elevated position symbolises that light, by means of fire, has been restored to the Candidate in order for him to perceive Masonic symbolism.

The Candidate is then placed in the North East corner of the Lodge in what can only be described as a most awkward position. He is instructed to place his right foot down the Lodge, his left foot across the Lodge, and to slightly turn his head to pay attention to the Worshipful Master. This somewhat awkward position has logic and history. In the old ceremonies of yore the Rough Ashlar which is an unhewn stone that represents the mind of the Entered Apprentice as it is, at this time, rough and unpolished by Masonic Wisdom and teachings. This stone, or an enlarged representation of it, was placed in the North East corner of the Lodge Room, and the Entered Apprentice in those days was placed tight up against it, and the stone being more or less square, his feet would have to follow the modern verbal instruction which is now given, as the stone has now been placed on the pedestal of the Junior Warden. This change to the original workings leads to various romantic reasons given for this once obvious action.

Here the Worshipful Master explains the main cornerstone of Freemasonry, which is Charity. And the Candidates attitude towards this admirable quality are tested and the extent to which it is practised within the Fraternity is detailed. Then the working tools of the degree are explained in both their actual use and moral implications. The Candidate then retires to restore his personal comforts and on his return is addressed with a magnificent Ancient Charge, parts of which I will be addressing as we progress in our explanations. That is the basics of the Entered Apprentices' Degree or First Degree of Freemasonry. Perhaps now would be a good time to explain some general aspects of the Lodge Officers work and some of the more unusual words of the First Degree.

The sign that rarely gets given correctly is the sign of approval when showing your agreement to a proposition or resolution. This sign is so important that I am amazed that its relevence is ignored. The sign of approval should be given by extending the right hand and arm out horizontally in front of the body, with the thumb and fingers in the form of a square. It is in this fashion that the right arm and hand are placed on the VSL when taking your obligations and firmly indicates that you are a man of honour, and as such you are confirming your support to the proposition. How many times have I witnessed just the hand held up, or Brethren given a simple "thumbs up". Such action simply removes the importance of any approval and that the proposition requires a firm and serious affirmation. Let's get it right, and let the newer Brethren see exactly how things should be done.

CHAPTER THREE

LODGE OFFICERS, AND LODGE WORDS

Over the past 250 years Freemasonry has changed very little, whatever changes have been made, have been relatively minor. The most dramatic being the re-location of the symbolic penalties of each degree. This was done to assuage predominantly pressure from the Church and changing public attitudes.

Over the same period, Society has changed drastically, socially, politically and economically, thereby widening the gap of non-understanding between the community and Freemasonry, creating, as we have witnessed recently, further mis-understanding and mis-information regarding our beloved Order. To such an extent that Grand Lodge, in its wisdom has decided to become a little more forthcoming, and wherever necessary and prudent to dispel any myths or misconceptions which may abound through lack of knowledge, without disturbing any of the traditional tenets and landmarks of the Craft.

Supply a better understanding and you create a greater interest for going further. Questions are simply a request for understanding and knowledge. Questions always indicate an interest. Fan that interest to a sensible, logical satisfaction, and you will have an ardent enthusiastic Mason.

This can be done at a domestic level, and it will run parallel with the modern attitude of Grand Lodge, who have the greater capacity to administer to the wider populace.

I shall now proceed, hopefully, to lighten a little more darkness, or at least clear a little mist and dispel a few mis-conceptions within the first degrees.

After having "come down" from the euphoria of the ceremony of my own Initiation and the Festive Board, I went home and began to study the summons I had been given during the ceremony. I examined the list of Officers, who had so perfectly, (I realised later) performed my Initiation. Naturally they were listed from the Worshipful Master downwards.

WORSHIPFUL MASTER !, fairly simple to reason, being in control of the Lodge, naturally titled Master, and as I reasoned that, although not worshipped in the religious sense, he was regarded, and rightly so, with respect and reverence.

Next came the IMMEDIATE PAST MASTER, this title explains his position admirably.

Following on, we come to the SENIOR and JUNIOR WARDENS. Wardens being guardians of doors, gates and rooms, it seemed logical to me that they should be the ones immediately answerable to the W.M., and as there is a Senior and Junior Warden, it naturally followed that there must be two rooms, gates or doors to safeguard or "WARD" off intruders. This was later confirmed when as a Fellowcraft I heard the lecture on the 2nd Degree Tracing Board.

In olden times DEACONS were carriers of messages, their functions being very well detailed in the ceremony of opening the Lodge.

Proceeding on, I came to the most self-explanatory of all the active Officers:- the INNER GUARD, who does exactly what his title implies.

The rest of the Officers, such as CHAPLAIN, ALMONER etc., are as with the Inner Guard, namely precise in their job description.

Last, but not at all least, we come to the Tyler...

.."TYLER" ???. This I have already fully explained in an earlier part of this book.

It must be borne in mind that, although unrealised and appreciated by many, it is a matter of recorded fact that the ONLY offices derived from the regulations laid down in the Ancient Landmarks, are the Master, his two Wardens and the Tyler !! The Deacons being fairly modern innovations, and the Inner Guard being the most modern innovation.

The earliest recording of a Deacon is Industry Lodge No.48 in 1734, it was two officers – Senior Deacon or Steward, and, Junior Deacon or Steward. In 1743 another Lodge recorded "a Masters Deacon" and "a Wardens Deacon", but they were not generally known until 1809 when the Lodge of Promulgation resolved that "Deacons were useful and necessary Officers".

I have often been asked to explain that part of the Senior Deacons duty that quotes; "and awaits the return of the Junior Deacon". This can easily be demonstrated, as I have done many times in many Lodges. The Worshipful Master gives a message to the Senior Deacon to be passed to both his principal assisting Officers, i.e. The Senior and Junior Wardens. The Senior Deacon then takes the message direct to the Senior Warden, gives it and remains standing by the Senior Wardens pedestal. The Senior Warden then passes the message to the Junior Deacon with the instruction to further pass it to the Junior Warden. This the Junior Deacon dutifully does and returns to his place and confirms to the Senior Warden that the message has been passed and all is well. The Senior Warden then passes this confirmation to the Senior Deacon who walks back to his position and confirms likewise to the Worshipful Master.

The earliest mention of the Inner Guard is in the minutes of Burlington Lodge No.96 of the 14th December 1814, but under the constitution the first mention was not until 1815. Before the creation of the office of Inner Guard, the duties were carried out by the Junior Deacon, and before that by the "Junior Entered Apprentice". Which brings me to the anomaly of the Inner Guards jewel of office.

The Tyler has as his Jewel a Sword Pendant (Hanging down). This aptly illustrates his duty and office, as do most of the Officers Jewels. He has a Sword which is part of his function and duty. The Inner Guards' Jewel has TWO Swords crossed and pendant, which would imply that he should have two swords and a doubly important role. But in reality he does not have occasion to use a sword. He does have occasion to use the poignard, but that is for a single specific purpose and is not a primary function, and anyway the poignard is not actually his, but part of the Lodge furniture, just like the working tools; and I believe he should not leave his situation to hand the W.M. the poignard during the ceremony of Initiation. He should remain where he is instructed during his investiture, "within the entrance of the Lodge". The Senior Deacon is the W.M.'s bearer and messenger. In olden times the Jewel appended to this task, which was then carried out by the Junior Entered Apprentice was a TROWEL!! Which implied the filling up of cracks and intercices etc., and knowing this, it now gives even greater impact and understanding to the phrase in the "Ancient Charge"....."they did not feel it derogatory to their dignity to exchange the Sceptre for the Trowel" The Sceptre being the highest emblem in the land, and the trowel being the symbol for the most subordinate office in the Lodge. Therefore the Inner Guard being fairly modern by comparison with the Tyler, comes inappropriately "jewelled", issued out of the human frailty of ignorance, and without the traditional historical role as that of the Tyler. Thereby confirming for me, the origins and authenticity of the Tyler's title. In this connection many Freemasons believe that the Jewel of the Charity Steward is a Trowel, but in reality it is not, it is a HEART. But because it has a small piece of metal attaching it to the collar of office it does resemble a Trowel....somewhat. But ask any Freemason..."What is the distinguishing characteristic of a Freemasons HEART?" and he will answer CHARITY.

Reverting back to the earlier point of "open air Lodges", the Master was traditionally placed in the East to represent the rising sun. The two Wardens or "Assistants" were both placed in the West. It was the duty of the Senior Warden to mark the setting sun. A stick was placed in front of the Worshipful Master to act like a sundial, "to mark the sun at the Meridian". When Lodges moved inside buildings, there was of course no shadow cast to mark the sun at the meridian. So the Junior Warden was conveniently placed in the South, which is the best place to observe the sun at the meridian. In modern ritual it is only the Senior Warden who is asked about his "CONSTANT" situation in the Lodge, logically implying that the Junior Warden was not constant, which of course he was not, as he moved to the south to assume the duty of marking the sun at its meridian for the W.M., who, being in the East, has his back to the Grand Luminary.

We are informed that our Lodges are, or should be, wherever practicable, placed East to West, like all churches or places of religious worship. All ancient holy buildings were constructed this way, not necessarily for any specific holy or religious reason, but purely for logical reasons, as, in those days there was very little or no artificial light, and from its construction, at times, precious little natural light. They were constructed to take full advantage of the natural light produced by that Grand Luminary, whose rising brings light and lustre through the large portals, which were left open to admit the same, so that it shone through to light up the altar and the religious dignitaries performing the ceremonies, so that the congregation could perceive without impediment. Therefore the entrance must have been in the East and the altar in the West. Our Lodges, appear to me, to be placed or inferred the same way. Therefore, it would appear that the Master is actually sitting in the West!! I leave you to cogitate on this apparent paradox. There is a popular Masonic Order that has the Worshipful Master sitting in the West.

And now we come to the meaning of some obscure words in the ritual. The word "COWAN" is quite ancient, and has a modern colloquial equivalent in "Cowboy", it literally means somebody who can do the work but is not formally qualified. The best definition of its early Masonic use is to be found in the minutes of Kilwinning Lodge No.0 in 1707, which recorded, "No Mason shall employ no Cowan, which is to say without the word to work", this means that a Cowan was a man who could do the work of a Mason but had not been given the "Masons Word"., thus debarring him from membership of a Lodge. I suppose the modern equivalent would read "No employer may employ a person without the proper authenticated qualifications", a bit like a Union protecting the employment of its members. The Knights Templar pop up again with a possible explanation for the origin of this word, In Gallic a bumpkin or idiot is known as COUENNE, pronounced "KOO-WAHN", again it does not take a great leap of faith to see a connection. And a bumpkin or idiot is not the sort of person you would like to learn of secrets that might cost you your life.

The word "HELE" is Anglo-Saxon in origin, and is still in use today in some parts of Cornwall. When a builder has completed the roof of a cottage or small dwelling, he announces the property is now "HELED", which actually means "covered", so we "cover, conceal, and never reveal".

The word "MOTE" is the third person singular of the subjunctive Anglo-Saxon word "MOTAN", which means "to be allowed", so we "allow it to be".

"PROFANE" is from two Latin words: "PRO", which means "in front of" and "FANUM" which referred to the temple, therefore the "PROFANE" were those outside the temple, or outside the "influence" of the temple. One can usually make a good guess as to the meaning of these obscure words from the context in which they are used, but how much better it is to actually know the true meaning.

Over the centuries words and their meanings and applications change, sometimes to such an extent as to mean almost the exact opposite to that of their origin and use, even in our lifetime. When we were teenagers anything WICKED was something evil and nasty, but to today's teenagers it means something fantastic and great. Imagine, if you will, a high society gathering some 200 years ago. Some of the men of this class would be gathered in groups, dressed in their frocked coats, breeches, hose and buckled shoes, discussing Masonic subjects discreetly behind their perfumed lace handkerchiefs, and would be deemed, by the uninitiated, to be ignored as they are "full of the Craft" or "full of the Art". Both these phrases have been modified, over the centuries, to one word and to apply in more general terms to anyone acting furtively or surreptitiously, as "Artful" or "Crafty". Both origins being lost in the mists of time.

The word "CANDIDATE" suffers to some extent from this malaise. Over the years it has come to lose some of its original specific application, as it is now applied to any newcomer or applicant, for any purpose, but its original meaning had a special significance to Freemasonry.

For research purposes we should only consider the first syllable, as the balance is a fairly modern appendage. It began, probably 4,000 years ago with a Sanskrit root word which we do spell as "CAND", which means "to shine", as when the light shines. With slight variations in spelling it has continued in this use ever since. The ancient Greeks called a glowing coal "Kinduras", remark on our word "Kindling". The Latins used the word "CANDIDUS" to denote something white and glowing, from it we have such words as "CANDLE", "CANDESCENT", "CANDID", and finally into "CANDIDATE". Among the Romans, a seeker for public office wore a bright white toga, to signify that he had pure intentions and nothing to hide. A candidate for Freemasonry comes similarly attired. Therefore with the original definition in mind i.e. shining whiteness and purity, it is for the Candidate to ensure that his record which is to become represented by the white lambskin, never becomes "STAINED" or "POLLUTED".

Coincidentally, the Knights Templar used to wear pure white lambskin under their tunics.

The word Architect promotes many a discussion, and if broken down and analysed, for me, is then clear and distinct, and therefore unarguable. The first syllable "Arch" specifically means superior or "Master", as in Archbishop, Archdeacon or Archduke, designating a "superior" or "Master" bishop, deacon or duke. When translating words which were applied centuries ago, you must not fall into the trap of applying its modern interpretation. The last syllable "Tect", comes from the word "Tectonics", which is the art of building, from this we get technician and technology. Therefore "Architect" literally means "Master of the Art of Building", exactly what was intended.

The words "ANNO LUCIS" means "In the year of Light" and, like the Jews, Freemasons measure time from the supposed creation, generally viewed to be 4,000 years before Christianity

"ASHLAR" is from the Latin "Axillaris", meaning Board or Plank. Within the old temples or tabernacles, the insides were adorned with timber from the ACACIA TREE, and obviously the planks were rough before they were smooth. Just how and when this word became applied to stone, I have no idea. The word "ACACIA" is the Latin botanical name for the Shitta or in the plural Shittim tree, from which the timber was used for the Tabernacle, The Ark of the Covenant, The Table of Shewbread, and the Furniture for the Holy Place. The wood is heavier than water, and is never attacked by the white ant or any other insect, and should not be confused with the "ACACIA BUSH", or as it is more popularly known in the U.K. as the Mimosa. The original "ACACIA" bush grows in the Desert of Sinai, and has bright orange flowers. When the desert sun shines full blast on it, it does appear as if, in the shimmering heat, that it is aflame and is burning, but being a sort of mirage, the bush is not actually consumed. Hence the local name of "the bush that burns" or "burning bush". It was at this same bush that Moses heard the word of the Lord. I will leave you to decide on the actualities of this apparent miracle or whether it was yet another mis-translation by the Greek translators of the original Bible.

The pavement on which we do all our work is called the "MOSAIC". This literally translates as "in the style of Moses". It is widely accepted, according to the Old Testament that Moses was responsible for the building of the 1st Tabernacle, at the foot of Mount Horeb, in the Sinai Desert, which was made from goat skins etc., so he searched around for stones to give the floor a more suitable reverence, by laying them in a pattern. So now any patterned stone work is called "MOSAIC" after that ancient event. As the word Judaic means "in the style of the Jews, and the term Archaic means, in the style of the Ancients, Mosaic means "in the style of Moses. Some say the pavement represents good and evil, night and day etc., with two such distinct opposites as black and white, you could make them represent any two opposites you choose.

Once again we have the Knights Templar possibility returning to the scene. As well as the banner of the Cross, they also carried a square banner divided horizontally, the bottom half black and the top half white, signifying the purity of the Christian ideals reigning supreme over the dark evils of the infidel.

Even the words Freemason or Freemasonry themselves have been the subject of much speculation. The majority take its literal sense to mean "Masons that are free from the Operative Bonds, and therefore free to moralise and expand on the specifics of practical Masonry". If this is accepted, then you have a paradox!! In so far as that we must all be COWANS, practising the profession in some form without the requisite qualifications.

STEPPING OFF WITH THE LEFT FOOT!

Freemasonry claiming an affinity with Ancient Egypt, it comes as no surprise to learn that all the statues of the Pharaohs of Egypt are depicted with their left foot first, for strength and victory. The armies of the world start marching with the left foot for the same reason. Interestingly the phrase "wrong-footed" is originally a particularly Egyptian phrase.

The "STEP" in Freemasonry has been the subject of many a discussion, but I have found that the most logical explanation is that it is an emblematical representation of the "TAU CROSS", shaped like a letter "T", and regarded to be the most perfect figure in Geometry. This reference will be familiar to many of you involved in other degrees in Freemasonry. One can imagine the moral speculation that could be produced on this perfect shape being considered the "rectitude of your actions". Yet again if you look at the persecution of the Knights Templar, one of the points on the list of "Heretical Acts", allegedly performed by them as part of their ritual, was that in the process of making this step "they trampled on the cross of Christ", which I have already fully explained. An accusation difficult to comprehend in these modern times, but not so in those far off religiously fanatical days. The cross of Christ is now generally accepted to be a "T" bar cross, and not the artistically represented one with the extended upright. Support for this interpretation of the "Step" can be seen in the W.M.'s. Apron. The three emblems are thought by so many to be levels, this cannot be so, as the level is the symbol of the Senior Warden. They are three TAU's, indicating that three steps have been completed: and if you put the three TAU's together you form what is called "THE TRIPLE TAU", a figure important in Royal Arch Masonry. In olden times, you could only join the Order of the Holy Royal Arch if you were a Past Master, and had completed those three steps. It must be fair to add that in olden times there were only two degrees, that of Entered Apprentice and that of Fellowcraft and the third step was the Masters Chair. Now that we have an actual third degree, you are now eligible for entrance into the H.R.A. once you have been a Master Mason for four weeks and upwards. Although the system has changed, the symbolism has not; this can lead to misunderstanding and misinterpretation.

SQUARING THE LODGE

Squaring the Lodge is deemed, by many, to be of a geometric tradition, symbolic of the perfect lines and angles of the square. But in reality it has developed from simple expediency and logic, and a desire to keep the Lodge tidy. In the old ceremonies the Tyler used to trace the Masonic Symbols and relative Lodge items in chalk, on a flagstone floor, and with pinned tapes, if on a wooden floor. So as not to "scuff" out his "Artwork" or dislodge his carefully pinned tape markings, an edge of about 18ins. was left around the outside for the perambulations to occur. When these tracings were placed on boards the habit or tradition of perambulating around the outside edge or "squaring" was maintained by many Lodges. Squaring has no more traditional significance than this. There are too many Masonic writers with an over-developed tendency to romanticise and spiritually speculate on the most simplistic aspects of the ritual, which tends only to confuse!

THE VOLUME OF THE SACRED LAW

I am often asked what is the correct way for the Volume of the Sacred Law to be placed. In giving my answer I have no desire to tread upon any Lodges' traditions, but if asked a question I must answer with logic and truth. The position of the Volume of the Sacred Law should be placed so that the Candidate can read it, and the other two Great Lights placed on the left hand page with the points of the compasses and the point of the square pointing toward the WEST. No, No, I hear you cry, it should be for the Master to read. In my view that is so wrong, as I will now explain. Under normal circumstances it will take about 9 years for a Master Mason to go through the offices of the Lodge and achieve that greatest of all honours "THE MASTERS

CHAIR". The attribute that the Worshipful Master represents, having reached that lofty position, is actually WISDOM, as the Senior Warden represents Strength, and the Junior Warden represents Beauty. If the Worshipful Master has not acquired sufficient wisdom, by studying the Volume of the Sacred Law and thereby making a daily advancement in Wisdom, during his journey to the Chair, then, surely, he is not worthy of occupying it. The Volume of the Sacred Law must be for the Candidate to read because he is without Masonic Wisdom and needs to acquire it through the pages of the Sacred Volume. If a Candidate of a different religious persuasion to Christianity is being initiated then he has the right to have the Holy Book of his choice placed on the pedestal, and I am sure that it would not be placed so that the Master could read it. In all probability it might be the Koran or the Hebrew Bible or some other equally different Holy Book, and the Master will most likely not be able to even understand it. To clinch this view, most Lodges, when the Blindfold is removed from the Candidates eyes and he is restored to light, firmly keep his head facing down towards the Volume of the Sacred Law. It cannot possibly be so that he can read it upside down!

How can the WM say "Let me direct your attention to what we call the Three Great Lights in Freemasonry", if they are upside down to the Candidate. That appears as nonsense.

In the old Craft ceremonies and indeed in many of the side orders today, the Holy Book is placed on a pedestal that sits in the middle of the Temple, and the Master is unable to read it. The Candidate is brought up to the pedestal, in the middle of the Temple, kneels and takes his Obligation accordingly.

Also the Volume of the Sacred Law should be open at Kings or Chronicles which depicts the building of King

Solomon's Temple so that the Candidate can read on what he has taken his Obligation, and not just any old place, which is so often done. So little attention is paid to this Great Light in Freemasonry that it's important relevance is sometimes innocently side-tracked.

THE WARDENS COLUMN OF OFFICE

(The columns of the Senior and Junior Wardens that enjoy placement on the respective pedestal should not be confused with the columns that represent the Three Lesser Lights.)

As the Deacons have "Wands of Office", so the Wardens have "Columns of Office".

Each of the Wardens' columns has a simple but distinctive role to play within the Lodge workings. In the old operative lodges the Wardens role was that of supervising the work, which is a role that has continued symbolically in our speculative lodges.

With the introduction of a second or "Junior" Warden, it became necessary to distinguish between their respective duties.

As, by the traditions of the Operative Lodges, the Senior Warden was in charge of the work or labour, so this aspect was continued in the Speculative Lodges and was signified by the upright position of his column of office.

In this regard the Junior Warden was appointed the responsibility of supervising the refreshment break and ensuring that the Fellows of the Craft returned, on time, to the labour of the Lodge. This duty had to be signified in a similar manner to that of the Senior Warden, hence the raising and lowering of the respective columns at the appropriate times.

Many Freemasons are unsure of which Warden has which column, and surprisingly, in my experience, so are a few Tylers. The simple logic applied to each is a sure way of never forgetting which column goes where. The Junior Warden marks the sun at its highest point, therefore under that bright light one can clearly see the land, but can never see the stars. Therefore the column with the Terrestrial globe on top is the one that goes on the Junior Wardens pedestal. The Senior Warden marks the setting sun, or even the moon, which is when one can readily see the stars. Therefore the column with the Celestial globe on top is the one that goes on the Senior Wardens pedestal.

Although many believe, and in fact, some infer, that the Wardens' columns have a greater signification than that explained above, this is not the case. Like many aspects in Freemasonic symbolism the reality is a simple logic far removed from the more romantic speculations.

In many Lodges the Wardens Columns carry the ornate pillar designs of the respective order of architecture that they are assumed to represent, namely Doric, Ionic and Corinthian, but logic tells me, and indeed shows me very clearly, that this assumption is totally incorrect, and has probably been added by some over enthusiastic wood carver, or an individual of a similar enthusiasm that passed such an instruction to the wood carver. The Orders of architecture that are revered and celebrated within the Masonic Ritual are amply illustrated on the Three Lesser lights that are prominently displayed on the right hand side of the Worshipful Master's, and the Senior and Junior Wardens pedestals. The Wardens columns of office should not display a similar embellishment. I will explain the logic of my statement.

A casual perusal of each of the Wardens columns will yield a glaring display of a globe atop each one, precisely representing those displayed on the 2nd Degree Tracing Board, and detailed in the appropriate lecture. Therefore as they represent these 2 magnificent pillars that were cast under the supervision of Hiram Abiff, and adorned the entrance of King Solomon's Temple, a structure created many centuries before the strict Orders of Architecture were so named, it must be most unlikely that the adornments so often embellished on these columns would not have been so created and so named. I am sure that the Egyptians and Hebrew builders would have been fully aware of the mathematics and stress allowance calculations necessary for the pillars to perform their allotted task, but they would have been adorned with their own embellishments such as the pomegranates and the lily-work etc., and not those of much later civilisations. I have continued with an extract from the Masonic lectures that I trust makes this point clear.

"In the history of man there is nothing more remarkable than that Masonry and civilisation, like twin sisters, have gone hand in hand; the Orders of Architecture mark their growth and progress. Dark, dreary and comfortless were those days when Masonry had not laid a line or extended her compasses; the races of mankind. In full possession of wild and savage liberty, and mutually afraid of offending each other, hid themselves in thickets of woods, in dens and caverns of the earth. In those poor recesses and gloomy solitudes Masonry found them, and T.G.G.O.T.U., pitying their forlorn situation, instructed them to build houses for their ease, defence and comfort. The first buildings they erected were of the rustic or TUSCAN order, a prompt but artless imitation of simple nature; its column is seven diameters high, its capital base and entablature have but few mouldings, yet there is a peculiar beauty in its simplicity which adds to its value, and renders it fit to be used in structures where the richer or more delicate orders might be deemed superfluous. Yet, rough and inelegant as these Tuscan buildings were, they had the salutary effect of causing mankind to assemble together, and thus led the way to improvements in arts and civilisation; for as the hardest bodies will polish by attrition, so will the roughest manners by communion and intercourse; thus by degrees they lost their asperity and ruggedness, and insensibly became mild from a fierce and barbarous nature.

Masonry beheld and gloried in the change, and as their minds softened and expanded, shewed them new lights and conducted them to further improvements, so that the Tuscan buildings pleased no more; they aimed at something more dignified and noble, and taking their ideas of symmetry from the human form, adopted that as their model. This gave rise to the DORIC order; its column is eight diameters high, it has no ornaments, except mouldings, on either base or capital, its frieze is distinguished by triglyphs and metopes, and the triglyphs compose the ornaments of the frieze. The composition of this order is both grand and noble; it is principally used in warlike structures, where strength and a noble, yet rough simplicity are required.

At this era their buildings, though admirably adapted for strength and convenience, wanted something in grace and elegance to captivate the eye and give them an aspect more worthy the appellation of scientific productions, which a continual observation of the softer sex supplied, for the eye that is charmed with symmetry cannot be insensible to woman's grace and beauty.

This gave rise to the IONIC order; its columns nine diameters high, its capital is adorned with volutes, and its cornice has dentils; and history informs us that the celebrated Temple of Diana at Ephesus, which was upwards of two hundred years in building, was composed of this order. Both elegance and ingenuity are displayed in the invention of this column; it is formed after the model of a beautiful young woman of elegant shape, attired in her hair, as a contrast to the DORIC, which represents a strong robust man. Thus the human genius began to bud; the leaf and flower ripening to perfection produced the fairest and choicest fruit—every liberal art, every ingenious science, that could civilise, refine and exalt mankind, then it was that Masonry put on her richest robes and decked herself in her most gorgeous apparel.

About this time a new capital was invented by Calimachus of Corinth, which gave rise to the CORINTHIAN order; it is the richest of the five, and a masterpiece of art; its column is ten diameters high, its capital is adorned with two rows of leaves and eight volutes which sustain the abacus; this order is issued in all stately and superb edifices. Calimachus is said to have taken the idea of this capital from the following remarkable circumstance: accidentally passing the tomb of a young girl, he observed a basket of toys, covered by a tile, placed over an acanthus root, which had been left there by her nurse. As the leaves grew up they encompassed the basket, until, arriving at the tile, they met with an obstruction and bent downwards, Calimachus, struck with the idea, imitated it in architecture; the vase of the capital he made to represent the basket, the abacus the tile, and the volutes the bending leaves.

Yet not content with this, the utmost production of her power, Masonry held forth her torch, and illumined the whole circle of its arts and sciences, which induced the Romans to go still further, and gave rise to the COMPOSITE, so named from being composed of parts of the other orders. It has two rows of leaves of the CORINTHIAN, the volutes of the IONIC, and the quarter rounds of the TUSCAN and DORIC orders; its column is also ten diameters high; its cornice has dentils or simple modillions. This order is used in structures where strength, elegance and beauty are displayed.

Painting and sculpture strained every nerve to decorate the buildings fair science had raised, while the curious hand designed the tapestry and furniture, beautifying and adorning them with figures emblematical of MUSIC, POETRY, ELOQUENCE, TEMPERANCE, FORTITUDE, PRUDENCE, JUSTICE, FAITH, HOPE, CHARITY, VIRTUE, HONOUR, MERCY, and many other Masonic emblems, but none shone with greater splendour than BROTHERLY LOVE, RELIEF and TRUTH".

One can clearly see from the above that the more modern embellishments are again simply romantic additions which tend only to confuse and mislead the Brethren.

The explanation of the Seniors Wardens term:- "To see that every Brother has had his due" is not as many think as referring to the paying of wages. This was traditionally and masonically effected in the Middle Chamber as explained in the ritual.

If there was ever any argument or dispute among the Master Masons then the Senior Warden would ensure that every Brother had fair opportunity to put his point of view, or in other words, had had his due.

THE DEACONS WANDS OF OFFICE

In days long past the Deacons wands were crowned with Mercury/Hermes, the winged messenger, as the Deacons were/are carriers of messages. Those were replaced with doves carrying an olive branch in their beaks. I can only assume that this was effected to remain more in line with the Solomonic legend being portrayed and in keeping with the Old Testament Hebrew stories, rather than elements from other cultures. The dove with the olive branch symbolises the bringing of peace, and also relates to the Old Testament story of Noah and the Ark when he sent out a dove to find land and the dove returned with an olive branch in its beak confirming that it had indeed found land. The dove crowning the Deacon's wands, for those reasons, seems more appropriate.

THE LEWIS

I am often asked why the Lewis or the "A" frame is placed on the Senior Wardens Pedestal. Again the explanation is one of simple logic. The reason for using an "A" frame to assist in lifting heavy stones is simply because an individual or group of individuals do not have the strength to lift it unaided. So the "A" frame gives you strength. The Senior Warden represents Strength, as the Master represents Wisdom and the Junior Warden, Beauty. The symbol on the WM's pedestal that represents Wisdom is, of course, the Book of Wisdom or the Holy Bible known masonically as the Volume of the Sacred Law. That book that will guide him in all his paths, from his Initiation right up to his Installation. The symbol representing the Beauty of the Junior Warden is a little more obtuse. The Junior Warden represents the Sun at its Meridian or highest point, which is when you can see the full extent of God's creative BEAUTY.

To be technically correct the "Lewis" is actually the metal hooking device inserted into the Perfect Ashlar to enable lifting.

In French Masonry the Lewis is known as a "Louvee", which also refers to a wolf cub. Wolves are most often depicted as baying at the moon, which fits the Senior Warden as he represents "The Moon to govern the night".

It may well be that as this French word refers to a wolf cub, which is the male offspring of the wolf; it has come to mean a son or grandson of a Mason in our traditions.

Also the biological brother of a Freemason is known as a Martin. I have yet to discover the reason.

THE TRACING BOARDS

Originally the various objects and pictures that were used as aids for the ceremonies were drawn or traced on the floor by the Tyler, and when the ceremony was finished they were washed away by the newest Entered Apprentice. When Freemasonry began to go "upmarket", so to speak, these drawings were placed on boards, and naturally became known as "Tracing Boards", or Trestle Boards as they were Boards that were placed on trestles. Naturally, they were artistically enhanced according to the romantic nature of the artist, who may or may not have been a Freemason, and therefore some of the mystical or esoteric nature might have become lost. There are beautiful lengthy lectures and explanations detailing the items depicted on the Tracing Boards, giving their full actualities and their moral and spiritual implications. Unfortunately these are now rarely given; when they are it is usually a demonstration, not of the beauty and content of the written word, but of the reciting ability of the individual giving the appropriate lecture. A sad situation, when there is so much knowledge contained in those lectures.

THE ROUGH ASHLAR

This is now a small roughly hewn stone that is placed on the Junior Wardens pedestal, but originally it was a much larger stone or an enlarged representation of such a stone, and it was placed in the North East corner of the Lodge, as explained earlier. It is meant to represent the unpolished mind of the Entered Apprentice, which, being without Masonic knowledge is metaphorically so in this respect.

THE PERFECT ASHLAR

The perfect ashlar is a perfectly hewn smooth stone and originally represented the polished mind of the Fellow Craft, as there was at that time only two degrees within the Craft Ritual. This was placed in the South East part of the Lodge, similar moral lessons being assimilated for the 2nd Degree as that of the 1st Degree.

Now that both stones have been placed respectively on the Junior Warden and Senior Warden's pedestals, those moral lessons are now rarely recounted, but can be found in the old lectures if any Freemason wishes to avail himself of them.

THE TASSELLED BORDER

The border of the carpet that adorns most Masonic Temples usually represents the half diamond pattern found on the apron of a Holy Royal Arch Companion, as most Craft Temples are used by the Chapters for their ceremonies, so the Carpet serves a shared purpose.

The tassels that occupy the four corners of the carpet are said to mystically "tie" and connect the four cardinal virtues, namely PRUDENCE, TEMPERENCE, FORTITUDE and JUSTICE, and every Freemason should endeavour to "tie" himself to these by regularly practising them. An allusion can also be made to the prayer shawl used within the Jewish Faith, as it too has a tassel on each corner symbolising a similar attribute. The Hebrew prayer shawl is also usually black and white, as is the Mosaic pavement.

In dismissing the value of the Side degrees one is often quoted "Pure and Ancient Freemasonry consists only of 3 degrees, Entered Apprentice, Fellow Craft and Master Mason including that of the Holy Royal Arch." This simply describes the Freemasonry of the Moderns and Ancients when they united. The Moderns described their Ritual as being PURE, whist the Ancients claimed, naturally, theirs to be Ancient. They could just have easily said that "Modern and Ancient Freemasonry consists of only................." or even better "United Freemasonry consists of only............" This simply tells you what they do and is not meant to dismiss the value of, or knowledge that is contained in the other side degrees. In its own ritual the Craft quite clearly states that Freemasonry is a "Progressive Science". I trust I have now put this definition precisely where it should be.

THE "G"

Little reference is made to this letter which hangs from the very center of the Lodge ceiling. In fact the only real reference is when the Junior Warden is asked ".....what have you discovered?", and his reply is....."…..the Sacred Symbol" . Some believe that the "Sacred Symbol" refers to Geometry, as in Sacred Geometry, the majority of Masons believe that it signifies God. As I have mentioned before, and firmly believe, that whatever a Mason personally sees in his interpretation of the ritual, then that is what it is for him. It is only when that belief is attempted to be passed on to others that a problem of acceptance may arise. The reality behind this symbol can be seen for what it does mean, in all its glory, in a few Temples around the country, and especially at the United Grand Lodge of England. Originally this sign used to be the Hebrew letter known as YOD, This character resembles an elongated S, and can be found just above the entrance to the Grand Temple at Great Queen Street, also it can be seen in glorious technicolour on the eastern frieze in the center of the rising sun. This Hebrew character Yod is signified in our terms as the letter "Y", which is the first letter of the Hebrew tetragrammaton YHVH which is YAHWEH, as the Hebrew language is void of vowels, they are inserted according to the custom of the western translators. Masonically, and western grammatics dictate that the letter Y is interchangeable with the letter J, as in Yesu and Jesu, again no great leap of faith is required here to go from YHVH to JHVH, which is the western JEHOVAH. So originally the Sacred Symbol referred to the Hebrew God Jehovah, and in our Grand Lodge that original symbolism is still maintained.

THE ANCIENT MYSTERIES

There are many references in the ritual to the "Ancient Mysteries", but there is no clear definition as to what they are, or where they come from. My researches have found them generally accepted to be of:- OSIRIS (Egypt), MITHRAS (Persia), ADONIS (Syria), DIONYSIS, BACCHUS and ELEUSIS (Greece), DRUIDS (Gaul and Britain). And are best summed up in the words of PLATO, from whom we get the PLATONIC bodies:-

"The mysteries were established by men of great genius to teach purity, to ameliorate the cruelty of the Human Race, to refine its morals and manners and to restrain society by the obligations of Fraternity".

A better appraisal of the objectives of Freemasonry you would be pushed to find!!!

THE MAGEN DAVID

This symbol is more commonly and masonically known as The Shield of David or the Seal of Solomon, and can be found on the Flag of Israel. It is the most significant symbol of Judaism. It is two equilateral triangles interlaced one on top of the other. This symbol can be seen all over Freemasonry, sometimes overtly and often in a very subtle manner. It is often displayed on the border of the Masonic carpet, and in many other areas of a Masonic Temple. It is prolific in the United Grand Lodge of England. It is on the finger plate of every door in the building, including the doors in the lavatories. Finally it is part of the Breast Jewel in the Holy Royal Arch. A stronger indication of the Judaic influence within Freemasonry you would be hard pushed to find, outside of the actual ritual itself. This symbol is the most common symbol within Freemasonry, more so than the Square and Compasses.

This symbol, before being adopted by the Jewish nation was held and used by many cultures as some sort of lucky talisman, and indeed, in some areas is still so used.

THE SIGN AND PENALTY

The sign of an Entered Apprentice is so well detailed in the ceremony that I need not dilate on it here. The penalty is somewhat different. To have t. t. t. o. by t. root is virtually impossible. The root lies too deep for another hand to grasp it, but to have t. t. t. o. from t. root makes logical sense. Also to be buried in t. s. o. t. s. at l. w. m. where the t. regularly e. a. f. t. i. t 24 hs. Why is this penalty so terrifying? What is so fearful that it is worthy of being such a penalty? The answer is very simple but not obvious to us in our enlightened world. Centuries ago, when the ritual was being compiled Religion was all powerful, as our history so carefully relates. The thought of not going to Heaven was the absolute worst thing that could happen to anyone, surpassed only by the possibility of going to Hell. Land that was covered by water was not consecrated, so the possibility of being buried in unconsecrated ground was deemed as the doorway to Hell with no chance of reaching to Heaven. This is why this penalty was deemed so terrifying.

Now we must look at the second or Fellow craft's degree.

CHAPTER FOUR

THE FELLOW CRAFT DEGREE

Like any progressive system, Freemasonry is no different in this respect, and candidates for progression are given a test in order to determine their merit and ability in the former degree, and therefore their qualification to be honoured and received into the Fellow Craft or Second degree.

In olden times a separate "Lodge" was arranged just prior to the actual Lodge meeting, specifically for instruction in the principles and teachings of the respective degrees. This was done by what is known as Catechetical format, and is amply demonstrated in the "Old Lectures", which are readily available, and often mentioned, and have therefore no real need for me to go into here. These Lodges of Instruction, although they still bear that title, have now degenerated into simple Lodges of Rehearsal, and actual Instruction appears to have been sacrificed. This lack of instruction clearly explains the absence of Masonic knowledge and the great amount of mis-information that abounds throughout our Institution. It is my most ardent hope that this book will go some way in redressing this sad situation.

The candidate for the Fellow Craft degree is attending the Lodge which is duly opened for work in the First degree. At the appropriate time on the Lodge Agenda, the Worshipful Master announces that "Brother ??? is a candidate to be passed to the degree of a Fellow Craft, but it is first necessary that he give proofs of his proficiency in the former degree" The Masonic term for progression from the First to the Second Degree, is known as Passing, i.e. passing from the first to the second. The modern method of giving proof of proficiency is by a small catechetical question and answer session between the Worshipful Master and the candidate. The questions are quite few and reasonably simple these days. The one that I would like to address is the last question in this brief test. The question is:

"How do you demonstrate the proof of your being a Mason to others?"

The reply to this question is:

"By signs, tokens, and the perfect points of my entrance"

Every single Freemason under the auspices of the United Grand Lodge of England and possibly the affiliated Grand Lodges around the world will give this reply. But ask them what the perfect points of their entrance are, and very, very few will be able to answer. Again the answer is simple, logical and is fully explained in the "Old Lectures", in fact, the very first lecture referred to in the usual Craft Ritual book. I cannot really give it in full detail here, but would strongly encourage a reading of the "Old Lectures". The simple answer to this question is just three words which are; "OF, AT & ON". And are explained accordingly; "Of my own free will and accord, At the door of the Lodge, and On the point of a sharp instrument". So few Masons are cognoscent of the truth I wonder constantly what would be the reply if a newly admitted Mason asked the question, "What are the perfect points of my entrance?". What I wonder would be the ingenious and contrived reply given to hide their ignorance of the facts.

After he has answered these set questions the Worshipful Master then "entrusts" him with a password and pass grip, without which he cannot gain admission back into the Lodge. This password is based upon a biblical story that takes place during the Ammonitish wars, and is of particular importance to Freemasons, and I have an explanation which I feel explains its construction and use.

The word "Sh------th", leading from the first to the second degree, was originally S-----t that is without the two letters h. We are informed in the Tracing Board Lecture that it was used as a test word to distinguish friend from foe. And that the accused, because of "a defect peculiar to their dialect" could not pronounce it properly, but only pronounce it in the original form without the h's, and were subsequently discovered and dealt with accordingly. We are not told exactly what this defect was.

The ancient Jewish language has no vowels, just consonants; Vowels are inserted by translators according to tradition and custom. Hence the main reason for the many different spellings of names and titles in the Bible. In the Bible we first come across "ABRAM", later we read it as ABRAHAM, also his wife "SARA" becomes SARAH, this change has significance. As you know Abram and Sara were without children, then Sara, late in her life, becomes pregnant. This was regarded as a blessing and a precious "Gift from God", It is then that Sara becomes Sarah, and Abram becomes Abraham. We must ignore the vowels, as they do not exist. The insertion of the "H" symbolised to the Jews that this individual was "Breathed on by God". Anything that was considered holy or somewhat magical was deemed blessed "with the breath of God", and indicated in this way. Now corn planted and later yielding flour, and producing bread, the staff of life, could well be considered magical or holy, and sent by God, or more traditionally "breathed on by God", and indicated locally by the insertion of an "H". This modification would be, for want of a better term, a local slang adaptation, and would not be known by outsiders, and could be used as a fairly sure way of discovering their origin. Much the same way as if you asked someone what they did on Saturday nights, and the reply came back "Go t'Pub". You could be sure that they were not from the South of the country. This, for me, is the explanation of that phrase "a defect peculiar to their dialect".

The candidate is then led out of the Lodge in order that he may be prepared by the Tyler to take his fellow Craft or second degree. He is prepared in a similar manner as that of the first degree except that he is not hoodwinked, his left arm, breast and right knee are made bare and his left heel is again slipshod. The Lodge is then opened for work in the second or Fellow Craft degree in the usual manner. The candidate is admitted into the Lodge by the Inner Guard and the ceremony is proceeded with.

The Candidate is escorted around the Lodge in order that his preparation is seen to be correct and he is presented to each of the two Wardens in order that he may prove his status as an Entered Apprentice Freemason. This is usually done by the Junior Deacon presenting the Candidate with the words, "Advance to the Junior Warden as such, showing the sign, and communicating the token and word of that degree." This is nearly always said in more or less one breath, which is entirely incorrect and pays no attention to the grammar and punctuation marks. How it should be precisely done is, the Junior Deacon releases his guiding hand and says to the Candidate; "Advance to the Junior Warden as such,....." here there is a comma indicating a pause, and in respect to the words "as such", which is simply the old fashioned way of saying "like this", the Junior Deacon should demonstrate the step, this is copied by the Candidate, once done the Junior Deacon continues, "showing the sign", here again there is a comma indicating a further pause, here the Junior Deacon demonstrates the sign which the Candidate copies and cuts.

The Junior Deacon then continues with, "communicating the token and word of that degree", the Candidate complies and the Junior Warden responds accordingly. This same procedure is effected with the Senior Warden. The ceremony continues and the Candidate finally kneels on his right knee when taking his obligation, his right hand is again on the Volume of the Sacred Law, and his left arm is made bare for a particular reason. After he has taken the Solemn obligation pertinent to the second degree, the Worshipful Master informs him of the secrets of the degree, and further informs him of the objects of the degree and the duties of a Fellow Craft. The objects of the degree are for the Fellow Craft to research and study the hidden mysteries of Nature and Science. To use the wonders of science to assist him in understanding and appreciating the wonders of Nature, and the beautiful handiwork of the Grand Geometrician of the Universe, in other words the natural beauty of God's creative powers. To fully appreciate the wonderful beauty of Nature in all its physical glory and also its spiritual essence. God has given us the world and all its wonders and wants us to fully understand the harmony and balance of this precious possession that has been bequeathed to us. So much has been done to upset the natural balance of the world, the results of which we are now experiencing, that a better understanding of the natural world could not be a better objective. Also spiritually to put ourselves in harmony with nature in order that we can better appreciate the wonderful possession that has been granted to us, and I mean here the world, that we can understand and hopefully adjust the natural balance back to its former glory. The world is in our possession, and we must look after it. Remember that the ritual for this degree was written some 300 years ago, what did the educated creators and members of our system know then, that we in our day seem so ignorant of. If we cast our minds back to the early civilisations we can see that an understanding and full appreciation of all the wonders of Nature and its cycles including the movements of the planets and the heavens, were an important part of those civilisations, and perhaps the evidence now presenting itself to our civilisation is proving the ignorance that we give to the skills of those early civilisations and the important messages that they have tried to convey to us. They may have simply called the natural powers of nature, handiwork of the Gods, and given them names and descriptions to suit the variable powers of nature, but in essence their descriptions suit the knowledge of their time. In our time we have greater scientific knowledge, so this should make our understanding easier, but material greed has driven us to ignore the warnings. The teachings of the second degree are now, in essence, an important lesson for all mankind which has been handed down from time immemorial and found its way into the teachings of our Masonic Fraternity. How important this message is, is demonstrated by the fact that the vast majority of the whole world are now advocating it, the same message that has been the voice of much earlier civilisations, and has been quietly but assuredly taught within our Masonic system positively for at least the last 300 years. I should now get off my platform and get back to the book.

The candidate is then invested with a new apron which has two rosettes simply to imply that you have completed two degrees. These two rosettes form the base of a yet incomplete triangle, a geometric symbol common throughout Freemasonry with many interpretations. The flap is left down to symbolise the opposite element of fire, namely that of water or the flow of intellect. The newly invested Fellow Craft is then placed in the South East corner of the Lodge, where the duties and responsibilities of a Fellow of the Craft are related to him. Then the working tools are explained both in their practical application and their moral interpretations. The Candidate is then handed a set of questions, the answers to which form a small test to prove his worthiness to progress to the Third and final degree.

The Worshipful Master congratulates him and the new Fellow of the Craft takes his seat in a Fellow Craft Lodge. The Lodge is then closed in the second degree and reference is made to the letter "G" hanging in the center of the Lodge, to which I referred and explained earlier.

The signs and penalty of this degree are so well explained within the ceremony that, once again, I need not dilate on them.

CHAPTER FIVE

THE MASTER MASON'S DEGREE

The Lodge, having been opened in the first and second degrees, the Candidate is then presented before the Worshipful Master who proceeds to put the prepared questions, to which the Candidate must give the answers that he has memorised. This being effected the Candidate is presented to the Worshipful Master where he is entrusted with a new password and pass grip in order that he can gain access into a Master Mason's Lodge.

It is this password or rather it's import, that, in my experience, is most grossly misunderstood and applied. This password is well known to all Master Masons but the import is mis-interpreted by most Freemasons, and this wrong understanding is passed on and on without question. This is the very point I mentioned earlier about the Senior Mason having been in the Craft for 51 years, which now I will explain.

This important password has an import, like all passwords and key secret words in Freemasonry. The import or meaning mostly given for this password leading from the second to the third degree, is WORLDLY POSSESSIONS. Nothing could be more wrong than this import as I will now explain. Remember that the Candidate is going from the Second to the Third degree, therefore to follow and continue Masonic knowledge, this password should reflect either something of the actual or of the moral teachings of the degree from which he is progressing. I have explained in great detail that the teachings of the second degree are the hidden mysteries of Nature and

Science, and that it is about using the advances of science to put yourself in harmony with Nature and God's creative beauty. It can be deemed as the beginnings of your spiritual path in Freemasonry. Spiritually it is putting you in possession of the world, in other words giving you WORLDLY POSSESSION in the SINGULAR. Science contains the knowledge that can put you, in the words of 300 years ago, in possession of the world, in order that you can look after it and maintain its beauty and splendour for future generations. It certainly does not mean the ACTUAL possession of the world in the manner of a dictatorial despot, but spiritually and as careful inheritors displaying the very teachings and the ethos of the whole Masonic structure. The term WORLDLY POSSESSIONS refers to such things as your house, car, cd collection and all the other material things that one acquires in ordinary life. This meaning also applied to the material things of 300 years ago when the ritual was first developing. Yes, Worldly Possessions refers to material things, those things that should be furthest from a Freemason's heart, and should never come into his Masonic thinking.

Further proof for this interpretation can be found in many Craft ritual books. As we Masons know and appreciate many words in the detailed ritual books of the Craft are displayed in an abbreviated form, for example, when the word Secret is needed to be shown, it is sometimes abbreviated to S..... Whereas if the word Secrets, in the plural, is needed to be shown, it is sometimes abbreviated to S......s. And sign and signs would be displayed in a similar manner. Of all the ritual books that I have investigated, and there are quite a few, I have never seen Worldly Possessions abbreviated as W.....P.....s, I have only ever seen it as Worldly Possession, displayed as W.....P......

Whenever I have fully explained this anomaly in a

Craft Lodge lecture, I can literally see the expression on many faces displaying the realisation of the truth behind this common misunderstanding. I can literally see "the penny drop".

Once entrusted the Candidate is escorted out of the Lodge where the Tyler will prepare him for the Third degree.

Becoming a Master Mason is a great event in a Mason's career, and the ceremony reflects this tremendous achievement and event by being conducted and conferred in an extremely dramatic and impressive manner. To go into too much detail about the Third degree would be wrong, but there are a few things that I could explain without damaging the great surprise that lies in store for the Candidate.

Having been presented at the door of the Lodge by the Tyler, the Candidate is led into the Lodge with both knees bare as he will be kneeling on both knees for the obligation in this degree. The dramatic story is then told and acted out in a most profound manner. The story is about the Master builder and Architect of King Solomon's Temple, Hiram Abiff. This individual was responsible for many aspects of the building of the Temple, its design and construction. He was such a highly respected individual, that he became a close friend and colleague to King Solomon and another colleague, King Hiram of Tyre who sent labourers and materials to King Solomon. Hiram Abiff was also from Tyre and was sent by King Hiram to assist his great friend Solomon. So there was a great council of three of which only one was actually Jewish. The Masonic legend continues and details the death of Hiram at the hands of three Fellow Craft Freemasons who wanted to obtain the Master Masons secrets in order that they could command a higher wage. But because Hiram Abiff refused to accommodate their demand they slew him. Throughout this dramatic episode the Candidate represents the character of Hiram Abiff, and is symbolically slain and hurriedly buried by the three assassins hopefully to hide their crime.

The loss of so important an individual caused great concern among the senior Masons, especially King Solomon, as could be reasonably expected, and a search is made for the Master Architect. His body is discovered and brought back to Jerusalem for a proper and respectful burial deserving of one so highly esteemed. The three assassins are caught and summarily executed.

The purpose of the Temple was mainly to house the most important Jewish religious artefact, the Ark of the Covenant and other sacred objects. As well as a place of worship it was also where the religious sacrifices were made. The Ark of the Covenant, built by Bezaleel and Aholiab according to plans delivered by God to Moses, held the Mercy Seat, which was designed to receive the Spirit of God, known as the Bath-Kol, when he visited his Chosen People. One of the most important laws within the Jewish religious culture is that the name of their God is so sacred that it cannot be tarnished by the human voice; neither can it be written down. This name was held by the three Grand Masters of the Temple, viz, King Solomon of Israel, King Hiram of Tyre and Hiram Abiff, and was preserved by each holding an individual syllable. This way the Jewish commandment or law was upheld and the actual name of the Jewish God was preserved sacred. But with the death of one of the important three, the secret of communicating the name was subsequently lost. But, each one of the three main players placed a personal Jewel with their part or syllable engraved thereon, also in three languages, just in case one of those three should die or be killed. These Jewels, according to Masonic Legend, were placed in the most sacred part of the Temple known as the Sanctum Sanctorum where no-one, except the High Priest and the three Grand Masters, were allowed to enter. So it would appear that the secret method of communicating the name was lost to the Master Mason. King Solomon then substituted two words to replace the original word, and these two words have designated all Master Masons throughout the Masonic world ever since that event. These two words are to be maintained until such time as the true word is re-discovered.

The history behind the story depicted by the ceremony is then related in great detail and the working operative tools attached to the degree are explained and their symbolic moral interpretations explored. The candidate then retires from the Lodge to restore his comfortable every-day clothing and re-enters the Lodge to be invested with his Master Masons Apron. This long-awaited investiture should occur with as much ceremonial as possible. It is a great event in a Masonic career and should be celebrated as such. The Apron is very different from the Candidates first two aprons, this has three rosettes in triangular fashion with the point uppermost, symbolising the triangle in all its meanings. There is also a light blue border which takes its origin from the Old Testament with the instruction from God that Aaron should edge his garments with light blue to distinguish his priestly role. The Apron is further decorated with two vertical ribbons symbolising the two pillars detailed in a particular part of the ceremonies. Attached to these two tassels are seven chains. Seven being a very special number with many special symbolic meanings. To a Freemason no Lodge is perfect unless seven of the Brethren are present. There are many examples of seven indicating perfection or completeness. The Candidate completes his Master

Masons degree by seven steps. In a like manner, in many other Orders, the degree is completed with seven steps. In nature seven is common indicating completeness or perfection. The spectrum has seven colours, the seven ages of man, the seven deadly sins and graces. As the Masonic ceremonies depict incidents from Jewish history, religion and culture there are many Hebrew aspects demonstrating the use of seven. The world was created within seven days; King Solomon's Temple was completed in seven years. In those biblical times no Jewish oath was deemed complete or perfect unless made in front of seven witnesses. To complete this explanation of the power and use of the number seven, in the Jewish language the word for seven is Shebang, (my spelling) which is where we get our saying "The whole Sherbang" from, which means everything. Finally the Apron is secured by means of a buckle which is a Serpent indicating wisdom, as it is deemed that unlike the Entered Apprentice and Fellow Craft the Master Mason now has some Masonic knowledge and wisdom.

The Candidate is then entrusted with the secrets, signs and grips attached to the degree. He is then congratulated, handed the Book of Constitution, the By-Laws of the Province, the By-Laws of his Lodge,

It is at about this point that an explanation of the symbols on the Third Degree Tracing Board are explained, but, unusually the symbols of the secret Masonic Code are never mentioned, and I find this very strange. These symbols have been on this Tracing Board since its original design but are so rarely explained that I have experienced Masons of up to 50 years longevity in Freemasonry that never had the meaning and significance explained although they are in a very prominent position on the Board. To fully appreciate the significance of this code one must have a copy of the Masonic Code displayed in the back of the

Mark Ritual book. It is not a secret peculiar only to the Mark degree as this code used to be used in Craft Lodges many decades ago, hence its existence on the Craft 3rd degree Tracing Board. In essence it is a very simple "pig-pen" code of a schoolboy nature, but with one important difference. As the Solomonic degrees of Freemasonry are of the Jewish culture and history, the letters are written from right to left as that is the manner in which the Jews read, so the translation must be effected in a similar manner.

Emulation 3rd Degree T.B.

The unexplained characters pertain directly to this cipher, and when translated and read correctly, reveal some interesting factors.

The first 2 characters, at the top of the Tracing Board translate as C T, and are either side of the Point within a Circle, that being a point from which a Master Mason cannot err.

The next line, on the inscription plate on the Coffin translates as B A H

The next line, underneath translates as 0003 L A (The numbers being in exact "mirror-image" *)

The last line translates as B M   B M.

Reading them in the normal manner, produces little or even no sense at all, that can genuinely be applied to the Masonic Legend. But, as our ceremonies depict events of a distinctly Judaic origin, and realising that the Jews read from right to left, as opposed to our left to right, suddenly, sense invades our investigations.

The first line has had 3 distinct applications:

1)   CABLETOW, which can be instantly dismissed as this reads from left to right.

2)   TUBAL-CAIN, which can just as instantly be

dismissed as this is not the 3rd Degree, but "leading" from the 2nd to the 3rd.

3) THE CENTRE, being that point from which a Master Mason cannot err. This definition holds the most logic.

There is a logical argument between the 2nd and 3rd explanations, in that the Mark degree is supposed to be an extension of the Fellowcraft degree, so the use of the word leading from the 2nd to the 3rd could be applicable, but as you have to be a Master Mason to join the MMM, the 3rd explanation would seem more logical.

The next line, read right to left are the initials of HIRAM ABIFF. As it is he who lies in the Coffin.

The next line, read right to left, in precise mirror image, is the year ANNO LUCIS of his death.

*On the tracing Board this figure is written NOT backwards, but in exact "mirror-image". This method of "coding" was one of the methods used by the Knights Templar, to hide certain information from the eyes of the profane.

The last line, read right to left, are the initials of the two words you are all in possession of. Proving the reference only to the 3rd Degree, and underlining the logic of the application of the definition THE CENTRE.

As the Solomonic degrees of Freemasonry are of the Jewish culture and history, the letters are written from right to left as that is the manner in which the Jews read, so the translation must be effected in a similar manner. The Candidate finally takes his seat in the Lodge. He is now a full Mason, and in due time will receive a Certificate proving such. This Certificate is a sort of Masonic passport which he can take with him whenever he visits a Lodge where he is not known, whether that Lodge be at home or abroad, he will be most genuinely welcomed. Possibly one of the greatest pleasures of being a Freemason is wherever you go, whether in your mother country or in any recognised Lodge abroad, and there are literally thousands, you will be warmly welcomed and looked after.

Whenever a Lodge is "opened" in a higher degree, those Masons not qualified to remain and participate in that degree are invited to retire until such time as the Lodge is back in their qualifying degree, at which time they are called on again for work.

The Lodge is closed in the Third Degree, and any 2nd Degree Masons are re-admitted. The Fellow Craft degree Lodge is then closed and all Entered Apprentice Masons are re-admitted, and the work detailed on the Agenda of the Lodge is then continued.

After a Masonic meeting has completed all its work, the Brethren retire to share what is known as a Festive Board. This takes the form of a full meal with wine, toasts and speeches. After each toast there is a peculiar Masonic tradition known as Masonic Fire. There are many varying explanations of the history of this particular tradition, some of a very romantic nature and some of a most distinctly dubious origin. I have a Ritual from 1760 which gives an explanation of Masonic Fire and describes its reference and original style, and I have copied it here in its original wording so that you can get a real feel of its contents. It is then left to you to decide for yourself of its validity up against all the other explanations that you may have been given.

It is somewhat difficult to read as it is written in the English of the period, but with patience it is very informative. So as not to lose the flavour of the written word, I will quote verbatim from the section on Masonic Fire, but I have modernised the spelling.

"WHEN THEY SIT DOWN TO THE TABLE, THE MASTER IS SEATED IN THE FIRST PLACE ON THE EAST SIDE; THE FIRST AND SECOND ASSISTANTS ARE SEATED OPPOSITE HIM ON THE WEST SIDE: IF 'TIS THE DAY OF A RECEPTION, THE CANDIDATES HAVE THE HONOURABLE PLACE, THAT IS TO SAY THEY ARE SEATED ON THE LEFT AND RIGHT OF THE MASTER, THE TWO ASSISTANTS, THE SECRETARY, AND THE TREASURER OF THE ORDER, WEAR ABOUT THEIR KNECKS A BLUE RIBBON ON A TRIANGULAR FIGURE, BY THE MASTERS RIBBON HANG A RULE AND A COMPASS, WHICH SHOULD BE MADE OF GOLD, OR AT LEAST GILT: THE ASSISTANTS AND THE OTHER OFFICERS CARRY THE COMPASS ALONE. THE CANDLES THAT ARE PLACED UPON THE TABLES, MUST ALWAYS BE PLACED IN THE FORM OF A TRIANGLE; NAY, THERE ARE MANY LODGES IN WHICH THE CANDLESTICKS ARE OF A TRIANGULAR FIGURE: THEY ARE USUALLY MADE OF WOOD, AND CARVED WITH ALLEGORICAL FIGURES, ALLUDING TO FREEMASONRY. HOWEVER, THIS IS NOT UNIVERSALLY OBSERVED.

UPON THE TABLE ARE ALWAYS PLACED THREE, FIVE, SEVEN OR NINE DISHES, WHEN THE WHOLE COMPANY ARE SEATED, EVERYBODY IS AT LIBERTY TO CALL FOR HIS BOTTLE: ALL THE TERMS THAT THEY MAKE USE OF IN DRINKING ARE BORROWED FROM ARTILLERY: THE BOTTLE THEY CALL A BARREL, WATER AND WINE THEY CALL POWDER, WITH THIS DIFFERENCE, THEY CALL THE FORMER WHITE AND THE LATTER RED, THE EXERCISE OBSERVED IN DRINKING DOES NOT ALLOW THEM TO MAKE USE OF GLASSES; THEIR GLASSES WOULD BE BROKE WHENEVER THEY DRINK: THEY

MAKE USE OF BOWLS, WHICH THEY CALL CANNONS. WHEN THEY DRINK IN CEREMONY THEY USE THIS EXPRESSION, "GIVE US POWDER", EVERYBODY RISES, AND THEN THE GRAND MASTER SAYS "CHARGE": THEY HEREUPON FILL THEIR BOWLS AND THE GRAND MASTER SAYS, "HANDLE YOUR ARMS --- PRESENT --- FIRE!: THUS ARE THE THREE DIFFERENT ACTIONS WHICH THEY OBSERVE IN DRINKING DISTINGUISHED. IN THE FIRST, THEY LAY THEIR HANDS ON THEIR BOWLS; IN THE SECOND THEY HOLD THEM OUT AS IT WERE TO PRESENT ARMS; AND IN THE THIRD, THEY ALL DRINK. IN DRINKING THEY ALL KEEP THEIR EYES UPON THE GRAND MASTER IN ORDER TO PERFORM THE EXERCISE TOGETHER; AND WHEN THEY HAVE DRANK, THEY HOLD THEIR BOWLS OUT BEFORE THEM, POINT, THEN LAY THEM ON THE LEFT BREAST, AND AFTERWARDS UPON THE RIGHT, AND THIS IS DONE THREE TIMES" (Indicated by our modern point, left, right, three times). THEY THEN LAY THEIR BOWLS THREE TIMES UPON THE TABLE, STRIKE THEIR HANDS TOGETHER THREE TIMES, AND EACH MEMBER CRIES OUT THREE TIMES, "VIVAT". (Symbolised now by the 3x3 claps). THEIR DRINKING IN THIS MANNER MAKES THE PRETTIEST SIGHT IMAGINABLE; AND IT MAY BE SAID TO THE PRAISE OF THE FREEMASONS, THAT THERE IS NO MILITARY SCHOOL IN WHICH THE EXERCISE IS PERFORMED WITH GREATER EXACTNESS.

LET THE ASSEMBLY BE EVER SO NUMEROUS, THE MOTION OF ONE IS ALWAYS FOR THE MOTION OF ALL THE REST; NO ONE IS EVER SEEN TO BE BEHIND HAND; AND AS SOON AS THE WORD OF COMMAND IS GIVEN, THE EXERCISE IS PERFORMED WITH A UNIFORMITY THAT RESEMBLES ENCHANTMENT.

THE NOISE THAT IS HEARD, WHEN THEY LAY THEIR

BOWLS UPON THE TABLE IS VERY CONSIDERABLE, BUT NOT CONFUSED; 'TIS BUT ONE SINGLE STROKE, BUT IT IS STRONG ENOUGH TO BREAK ANY VESSEL NOT MADE OF SOLID METAL: IF ANYONE FAILED IN THE EXERCISE THEY WOULD BEGIN AGAIN, BUT THEY WOULD NOT FILL THEIR BOWLS A-NEW; THIS HAPPENS BUT SELDOM, BUT IT HAPPENS SOMETIMES: SUCH BLUNDERS ARE GENERALLY COMMITTED BY MEMBERS NEWLY RECEIVED, WHO ARE NOT ACCUSTOMED TO THE EXERCISE".

In respect to the modern question "Brother Wardens, how do you report your respective columns?" .This refers to columns of artillery and not the table columns or sprigs. And the reply "Fully charged in the west, W.M." etc., refers to the preparedness of artillery, and not the glasses being charged full of wine, although it is an excellent simile! The word "Fire!" is obviously self-explanatory.

Having completed all the Toasts and the speeches and the meal there is one final toast. This final toast is given by the Tyler. It is one that all Brethren become extremely familiar with but rarely appreciate its possible origin. As I have mentioned many times that the content of many Masonic Orders take their basis and ethos from events depicted in the biblical history of the Jewish nation. I will now quote a bit of traditional Jewish culture that still regularly occurs throughout Judaism worldwide. This takes place every Monday and Thursday morning within the Jewish Synagogue just prior to the Rabbi rolling up the Torah before locking it away. He recites a prayer that takes the format of:

"To all poor and distressed Sons of Mother Israel, where ere dispersed over the face of Earth and Water, wishing them relief from all there sufferings and a safe return to

Mother Israel, should they so desire"

Many of you will recognise this quote and perhaps will not be so surprised at the direct Jewish connection.

Such are the 3 ceremonial degrees of Craft Freemasonry. Having detailed each degree it is but fair to say that as well as the practical lessons of history contained in each degree there are also other aspects intertwined for those with "eyes to see", and for those with the inclination and interest for those other aspects.

Freemasonry is very much a collective, managed and conducted by individuals, and attractive to all sorts of individuals for many different reasons. Providing a candidate is well spoken for and vouched for he is most welcome. Many Freemasons enjoy a tremendous Masonic career without considering the more spiritual, moral or religious aspects of the Fraternity whatsoever, and there is nothing wrong with that at all. If what you see is what you want then Freemasonry has much to offer in this respect. But there is so much more awaiting the more curious and investigative Mason. Within the Masonic ceremonial there are many interpretations of the expertly phrased prose, many definitions of the masonic symbols, and deeper understanding of its intrinsic message. For those who are quite content to meet occasionally, conduct a ceremony and then dine within a most friendly and convivial atmosphere, there is much for them to avail themselves. Visiting other Lodges, whether within the same province or much wider afield, is always a great fulfilling occasion. Any contributions that these individuals make towards the Masonic charity ambitions, whether financially or with time and/or labour, it is equal to that of a Mason who is perhaps more interested in the deeper meaning of the ritual in either the spiritual or mystical elements.

The choice of the paths within the Freemasonic system available to every individual is many, and each path has its aims and objectives, and satisfaction, and are as short or as long as the individual wishes.

From this basic root of Freemasonry, known as "The Craft", many branches spread out. These branches will accommodate the more curious and investigative Mason, and can be summarily listed as follows.

The Solomonic degrees are those that continue the story and legend of the Temple, and particular incidents based on the biblical history of the Jewish nation. These Orders I would deem as: The Craft; Holy Royal Arch; The Mark Degree plus Royal Ark Mariners; Royal and Select Masters plus The Order of the Silver Trowel; The Order of the Secret Monitor plus The Ancient and Masonic Order of the Scarlet Cord; The Operatives, and the Knight Masons.

The Christian Orders are those that weave around the biblical story of Jesus, or historical events specifically related to Christianity. These Orders require a belief in the Christian Trinity, that is, Father, Son and Holy Ghost, One God. These Orders I would deem as: The Knights Templar plus The Knights of Malta plus Knight Templar Priests; The Red Cross of Constantine plus The Knights of the Holy Sepulchre and The Knights of St.John the Evangelist; Rose Croix; The Royal Order of Scotland; The Societas Rosicruciana in Anglia.

Referring back to my mentioning of the Esotericism to be found throughout the Masonic structure, there is one particular Order that can rightly be deemed as the beginning of your more serious and overt esoteric study, and that is The Societas Rosicruciana in Anglia. Although there are certain aspects of esoterica in all the Masonic degrees, the S.R.I.A. or SocRos as it is more familiarly known is generally regarded as being more overtly esoteric and spiritual, and is a solid base from which to explore and develop your interest in the more spiritual and mystical path in Freemasonry.

There are two Masonic Orders that are particularly regarded to be specifically English, and are The Commemorative Order of St. Thomas of Acon; The Masonic Order of Athelstan.

There are many, many Orders that proliferate the Masonic world, and, as is always the case, there are many that falsely claim an affinity to the "official" Masonic structure. It would be wise to avoid such groups. Personally I am involved in many of the former, and all the Orders that I belong to insist on a first important requisite that you must be a Master Mason under the United Grand Lodge of England. This I find as a great safeguard, as I know that everyone involved has the basic important teachings of the three degrees of Craft Masonry governed by UGLE.

Now I must return to the Craft and the source from which it obtains its teachings.

In the Craft, as is in much of mainstream Freemasonry, the source from which the basis of the degrees are developed is the Bible, mainly the Old Testament. This source, for centuries, was deemed to have been written by Moses himself, or at least the first five books were, which collectively are known as The Torah and are held in the highest esteem and faith by the Jewish religion. If the traditional belief of its author is held to be a fact, then the writings are millennia old. I say writings, but writing was a skill acquired by very, very few in Moses's time. Perhaps only the Priests and maybe a few wily merchants. The stories so precious to the Hebrew faith were recounted orally from memory and handed down by mouth to ear. One can imagine the errors that could be achieved by this method of communication. There was little point in writing as so few could read, and record keeping for posterity was not a practise widely observed in those times. It was not until some time in the first century AD that writings began to be made and records began to be kept. So it is a few millennia from the first supposed writings by Moses until the first recordings of these stories in the first century AD. One can only imagine how much romance, artistic embellishments and creative imaginings could have become added to the basic stories of the Creation, Flood, Garden of Eden etc. etc. by the time that they came to be recorded by scribes in the first century AD. These biblical stories so revered, so powerfully indoctrinated into the psyche of literally billions of followers, now form the faith of the three most powerful religions of the world. Here we have the Judaic Faith, the Islamic Faith and the Christian Faith. In the first two religions the basic principles of the respective faith form the basis of the Laws of the respective countries over which these two faiths have dominance, in the case of the third, the Christian Faith, of which I can only really talk about my own country, the judicial system of England is founded on Christian principles. Let me state here quite emphatically that I have no problem with any of this, in essence there is nothing wrong with the principles of any religion, where the problems arise is with the individuals that perhaps govern the religion or have great sway in the interpretation and implication of the respective basic principles of such. There is a great confusion these days with the overuse of the words Fundamentalists and Fanatics, so much so that the two have become blurred. A Fundamentalist is someone who strictly abides by the fundamental principles of his or her faith. It can justifiably be said that the Pope is a fundamentalist, Mohammed and Jesus were fundamentalists, a tremendous attribute that should be respected. A Fanatic is the exact opposite, and interprets his or her faith according their own principles and is determined to inflict that interpretation on all others. Because of this blurring and the current accent and focus that is currently being exerted on the faiths of the world, perhaps a closer look at the origins would yield the profit of a greater understanding of the relationship between religion and Freemasonic ritual and ceremony.

When the bible, or more correctly, the books that came to constitute the bible, were first being written on papyrus, goat and sheep skin, they were naturally written in the language of the writer and the style and form of that language and time. Centuries later a selective choice of these books was made by the Church fathers that then formed the original bible. The original books were translated from the Aramaic, to the Hebrew then into Greek and from there into Latin, the latter becoming the "official" language of the then dominant church. One must surely expect some, perhaps many, errors to occur in going from the first language and finally ending in the fourth language, which in fact many people of the congregation did not actually speak. We can be sure that some of the original intent and meaning became forever lost. At that time there were no actual copies available for any interested lay people to study, in fact so few could read that the need did not arise. Also there was little actual knowledge of the sciences and certainly no archaeology to enable even the least trace of any verification or support of the authenticity of the events recorded in the books of the bible. This situation existed for many centuries and meant that the only authority on those recorded biblical events was the body that selected them, and that body was the Church, or perhaps I should say the Roman Catholic Church. Obviously my concentration here is on the Christian religion as I am of that faith and can speak more knowingly on it, the other two, for obvious reasons, I do not consider to be my province in which to comment so freely.

This for many centuries was the religious system that prevailed and all contrary thoughts or opposing beliefs were violently put down by the ruling Church. Gradually, as I have already detailed, things began to change. After many struggles and persecutions the bible began to be published in English and subsequently other languages, and it must be acknowledged that a little more became lost in translation. Once this great volume began to become available and people could read and study, it naturally raised questions of interpretation. It is about this time that the format of the Masonic rituals were being formed. It must be appreciated that the rituals were formulated in the style, wording and knowledge of those times. Among some of the more well educated of the populace, differing thoughts and opinions began to be quietly expressed. These were gradually being supported and to a degree confirmed by the development of archaeology and the accompanying sciences. The Church began a vociferous campaign in defending their position and dogma. From those times, now expressed as the Age of Enlightenment, archaeology rapidly developed into the diverse science that it is today. Communication of knowledge developed at such a pace that intelligent progress began to overtake traditional assumptions and religious dogma. Discoveries of such artefacts as the Nag Hammadi and Dead Sea Scrolls and the academic study of them have encouraged fresh interpretations of biblical events, which in turn have focussed the attention of Masonic scholars and researchers, like myself.

We should all acknowledge that the Masonic rituals were created when total belief and acceptance of the biblical stories as written was paramount, archaeology was in its primitive and foetal stage, and suppression from the religious authorities of contrary views to their own dogma was all-powerful. Plus the very important fact that the bible itself has been "edited" eleven times since Henry the Eighth first had a contre-tente with the Pope, and ended up going his own way and forming the Anglican Church. This "editing" was finally ended by King James the First of England by the publication of his "Authorised Version" of the bible. Personally I feel that the "Authorisation" of God's Word, (which is what the bible is regarded by many to be), by an earthly king, is totally over the top, and gives the impression that the king is a higher authority than God himself. In fact, as one would expect it was not King James that actually did the editing, but it was a Freemason, an individual known as William Schaw, author of the noted "Schaw Statutes" on which much of our current rituals are based, a touch ironic don't you think considering the attitude of the Catholic Church towards Freemasonry. Therefore the treatment, understanding and interpretation of the rituals must be respected in the light that prevailed in those times. Nowadays no-one really believes that wolves dress up in their granny's clothes, but we all tell our children and our grandchildren the story of Little Red Riding Hood simply for the very important moral principle and warning that innocently appears to underline the story, and this is probably the best way in which to get this across to a young child that is without sophisticated knowledge or learning. If we consider this analogy to be synonymous with understanding the Masonic Ritual then it will go a long way to assist in obtaining the much greater meaning and lessons lying within the wonderful prose that forms our beautiful degrees and ceremonies.

THE DEGREE OF INSTALLED MASTER

After fulfilling the duties of all the offices that are
engaged on the floor and in the ceremonies of the Masonic
Lodge, one reaches the ultimate office and the highest
honour that any Lodge can bestow upon any of its members,
that of Worshipful Master. It is the highest office in any
Lodge, and, as the ritual dictates, the Worshipful Master
should rule and direct his Lodge. He should not allow
anyone else to rule and direct, but, having said that, it
would be a foolish Worshipful Master that did not seek
advice and guidance from those who have served the
Lodge longer. In my opinion the Worshipful Master should
not use the phrase "…..which is in the capable hands
of……", as whatever the matter may be it is in the hands
of the Worshipful Master alone and no one else. He can,
of course, call on any Brother to speak or advise on the
matter, such as Secretary, Treasurer etc. etc., as, apart
from the Treasurer and Tyler, every other Officer was
appointed by him in consultation with the Past Masters of
the Lodge, so the Master is ultimately responsible, and the
matters are therefore in his capable hands.

Another small point that tends to be overdone is the use
of the Gavel. The Gavel is quite rightly a symbol of power
and should be used to call the attention of the assembled
Brethren. If they are sitting quietly and awaiting the
next item then to use the Gavel would be superfluous
and therefore unnecessary and simply displays that it is
done out of habit and without the full appreciation and
understanding of its proper use.

Originally there were only 2 degrees within
Freemasonry, that of Entered Apprentice and Fellow
Craft, the Master Masons degree coming much later. So

the original ceremony of Installation into the Masters Chair was conducted from the Fellow Craft degree. This tradition, in part, is continued at the present time.

The ceremony conducted by most Lodges is the permitted "shortened" version and is so common that many Freemasons do not realise that the original full ceremony ever existed. Originally the Master Elect was entrusted with a password and retired from the Lodge whilst the Lodge was fully opened up in a Board of Installed Masters. The Master Elect then re-entered and the full ceremony was conducted with many signs and a full set of working tools. The Board of Installed Masters was then fully closed, and the Lodge gradually went down to the first degree and the Lodge Officers, having been appointed sometime earlier, were then invested and advised of their respective duties. It seems a great paradox to me that having quoted within its ritual how being Installed as Worshipful Master is the highest honour that any Lodge can bestow on one of its members, that it is so often effected within a shortened ceremony.

The Craft consists of 4 degrees, that of Entered Apprentice, Fellow Craft and Master Mason. As far as I am aware there is no permitted shortened version of the Entered Apprentice, Fellow Craft or Master Mason degrees, it is only the Installed Masters ceremony, the highest honour that the Lodge can bestow on any of its members, that suffers this paradox. Surely such a high honour deserves the full ceremony. I have seen the full ceremony and have been an integral part of conducting it, and I can give the greatest assurance that this full ceremony aptly suits the description of the highest honour that the Lodge can bestow,. I am therefore bewildered as to why more Lodges do not conduct this full ceremony. Maybe time has become the most important aspect of Lodge meetings and not the actual ceremonies or business of the Lodge.

The shortened ceremony takes the format of what one might expect for an Installation ceremony, so there is little need for me to dilate on it here.

There is one aspect that does require explaining and that is; Who is it, within the Masonic Legend that occupies the Masters Chair? When asked this question so many Freemasons reply that it is King Solomon. This cannot be so as, according to the ritual, he is "the humble representative of King Solomon", and therefore cannot actually be King Solomon. So who is he? The Installation ritual is quite clear on this point, and there are many indications in other Orders of the importance of this individual. It is ADONIRAM. He who is beckoned three times etc.etc. As mentioned earlier there were only two degrees in the Craft, that of Entered Apprentice and of Fellowcraft. The Mark degree takes it origin from the Craft second degree, and within that Order ADONIRAM rates high importance. Likewise within the Order of the Royal and Select Masters the close relationship between Hiram Abiff and Adoniram is further detailed, confirming for me the quote from Mackey's Encyclopaedia of Freemasonry that Hiram Abiff had married Adoniram's sister thereby becoming brothers-in-law. Within Jewish culture the close family relationships can be clearly seen and appreciated, even in modern times, and this close relationship of Hiram Abiff and Adoniram demonstrated in this Order of Royal and Select Masters exemplifies this precisely. In the Royal Order of Scotland ritual the reply to a question demanding who you are and from whence you came, the reply is "G....M is my title, Adoniram is my name, and from a just and perfect Lodge I came" .Freemasonry is a progressive science and there is so much to be learned from the other Masonic Orders if that is your inclination.

Having worked and studied the ritual of the degrees for usually 9-10 years, and completed his year as Worshipful Master, that being the highest honour that the Lodge can bestow on any of its members, the outgoing Master is invested with a Breast jewel that commemorates his successful year. This is known as a Past Masters Jewel. Although the Worshipful Master has worked extremely hard and well for his Lodge, and dutifully receives and proudly wears such a Jewel, very few Past Masters fully appreciate the true meaning of the symbolism that the Jewel purveys. The Jewel symbolises the 47th proposition of Euclid. This is a symbol containing a myriad of interpretations, but for the purposes of this explanation we will stay with the Craft. Euclid was credited with the discovery of this key principle of Geometry which was purported to have been proved by Pythagoras. But in reality the Egyptians and before them the Babylonians were well cognoscent of the formula but they called it by a different name – Plimpton 322. Pythagoras was well skilled in the mystical schools of the Egyptians and Babylonians which no doubt had a great influence on his confirmation of Euclid's proposition. The essence of the esoteric meaning of the proposition within the Pythagorean schools of thought was that everything within and without the universe had a numerical harmony and balance that could not possibly be a coincidence, thereby proving the existence of the GAOTU and his creative beauty. This Past Master's Jewel is certainly worthy of research and investigation as you work hard and long to earn its reward so it naturally follows that you should be able to fully appreciate its true value and meaning. I have given just a sample of its importance hoping that it will spur the recipient to make his own researches into this hard earned reward.

When presenting the Warrant to the newly installed

WM, the Emulation ritual categorically states that the Worshipful Master should be seated to receive it. This, to me, makes no sense and totally belies the quality of the ritual. The ritual clearly states the importance of a Warrant, that no Lodge can be opened in the absence of such a Warrant, and that it has been protected and cared for by all the Past Masters and is now presented in all its splendour having lost none of its previous lustre, etc., etc., Surely the recipient should receive it, and its importance, standing so that all the Brethren can clearly see that the Warrant is regarded in the manner in which the written word informs. Just a thought. It seems that most Emulation Lodges ignore this written instruction and present it to the standing newly Installed Master.

In a like manner, the Emulation book of ritual clearly states that when the investiture of the Tyler takes place, the Inner Guard should not be sent out to temporarily act as Tyler, he should remain where instructed, within the entrance of the Lodge. So many times have I seen the casual expediency of using the Inner Guard in this manner. The person that goes outside to temporarily act as Tyler should be a Past Master.

Many Freemasons do not fully appreciate that the Initiate has a token (grip) and a word. I do not mean that of an Entered Apprentice, I mean an Initiate, someone who has not yet even entered the Lodge. The Token is a regular handshake and the word is F.A.O.G. Report. This is the manner in which he is greeted at the door by the Inner Guard and likewise how he is presented to the Junior and Senior Wardens. Which is precisely how he is presented when passing from Entered Apprentice to Fellow-Craft, and when being raised to the degree of a Master Mason.

Being a very spiritual Freemason myself and very involved with the esoteric side of Masonic Orders, I must make a brief response to those Freemasons who claim that there is not only no place for spirituality but also that there is nothing esoteric within the Craft rituals. As in most things "beauty is in the eye of the beholder".

Numbers play a very important role in all the Freemasonic Craft ceremonies and I will detail just a small part by explaining the esoteric aspects of 3, 5 & 7.

The first 3 steps of the Entered Apprentice symbolise the creative powers of Wisdom, Strength and Beauty exemplified by the Deity during the Creation process. They also represent the 3 Cardinal points of the day namely, Sunrise, Midday and Sunset which are represented by the 3 principal officers, the Worshipful Master, and the Senior and Junior Wardens.

The 5 steps of the Fellowcraft denote the five principal elements created by Wisdom, Strength and Beauty and are essential for life on this earth, namely, Earth, Water, Air, Fire and Spirit. These also symbolise the 5 Officers that hold a lodge, namely the Worshipful Master his two Wardens plus the two Deacons.

The 7 steps of the Master Mason denote the seven stages of Creation, the seven planets and much more that I have explained earlier, plus, of course the seven that make a lodge perfect, the 5 Officers mentioned above plus the Inner and Outer Guards.

This is simply a small "taster" of the esoteric elements within the Craft rituals. There is so much more for those with "eyes to see".

In closing this detailed explanation of various aspects of the Craft I cannot recommend enough a close attention and absorption of the information contained in the investiture of the Officers of the Lodge. Rather than simply learning the ritual parrot fashion, understand it, see its meaning, then you are able to deliver it to the candidate in a way that perhaps he will be able to better understand.

I have many times stressed the importance of the other mainstream Orders within the Masonic system, in that they do confirm that freemasonry is a progressive science, and do contain much information that greatly assists in understanding the root of all Freemasonry, that is the Craft. If you purchase a book and only read Chapter One, then the rest of the book is lost to you, you will never discover if the Butler did it or if he didn't. Reading Chapter Two gives greater insight into Chapter One and so on. This simple analogy indicates the importance to any inquiring Freemason of the progression within the Masonic system. Having said that, it is not essential for everyone. Many are quite content with just joining the Craft, attending a meeting, appreciating a ceremony and having some time with his brethren over a nice dinner, knowing that his contribution to the aims and objectives in Freemasonry are as comparable to those of someone like myself, an avid researcher and historian, especially the donations to Charity.

Freemasonry is everything to everyone. The Craft is so varied in its structure that there is something, somewhere for each member. It may be administration, ceremonial, fund-raising, event organising or any of the other functions required for a masonic Lodge to run efficiently and smoothly.

I hope that I have brought you all something of interest and have assisted in expanding your Masonic knowledge so that you can better appreciate and understand our beautifully crafted ritual and ceremonial that illustrates our principles and objectives.

For me, without any doubt whatsoever, Freemasonry

makes my world a much better place, gives me an understanding that allows me better relationships with my fellow-man, whether they be Mason or Non-Mason. It also gives me a much better and more comfortable understanding of my relationship with my God, something that the Church could not achieve, and something that I struggled to find in my formative years.

I trust that you are as fortunate within your own Masonic Career as I have been in mine.

Ray Hudson
June 2013

Parchment Books is committed to publishing high quality
Esoteric/Mystic classic texts at a reasonable price.

With the premium on space in modern dwellings, we also strive - within
the limits of good book design - to make our products as slender as
possible, allowing more books to be fitted into a given bookshelf area.

Parchment Books is an imprint of Aziloth Books, which has established itself
as a publisher boasting a diverse list of powerful, quality titles, including
novels of flair and originality, and factual publications on controversial
issues that have not found a home in the rather staid and politically-correct
atmosphere of many publishing houses.

Titles Include:

Secret Doctrines of the Rosicrucians	Magus Incognito
Corpus Hermeticum	GRS Mead (trans.)
The Virgin of the World	Hermes Trismegistus
Raja Yoga	Yogi Ramacharaka
Knowledge of the Higher Worlds	Steiner
The Outline of Sanity	GK Chesterton
The Most Holy Trinosophia	St Germaine
The Gospel of Thomas	Anonymous
Pistis Sophia	GRS Mead (trans.)
The Teachings of Zoroaster	S.A. Kapadia
The Mystical Qabalah	Dion Fortune
De Rerum Natura	Lucretius

Obtainable at all good online and local bookstores.
View Aziloth's full list at:
www.azilothbooks.com

We are a small, approachable company and would love to hear any of
your comments and suggestions on our plans, products, or indeed on
absolutely anything.   Aziloth is also interested in hearing from aspiring
authors whom we might publish. We look forward to meeting you.
Contact us at: info@azilothbooks.com.

CATHEDRAL CLASSICS

Parchment Book's sister imprint, Cathedral Classics, hosts an array of classic literature, from ancient tomes to twentieth-century masterpieces, all of which deserve a place in your home. A small selection is detailed below:

Mary Shelley	*Frankenstein*
H G Wells	*The Time Machine; The Invisible Man*
Niccolo Machiavelli	*The Prince*
Omar Khayyam	*The Rubaiyat of Omar Khayyam*
Joseph Conrad	*Heart of Darkness; The Secret Agent*
Jane Austen	*Persuasion; Northanger Abbey*
Oscar Wilde	*The Picture of Dorian Gray*
Voltaire	*Candide*
Bulwer Lytton	*The Coming Race*
Arthur Conan Doyle	*The Adventures of Sherlock Holmes*
John Buchan	*The Thirty-Nine Steps*
Friedrich Nietzsche	*Beyond Good and Evil*
Henry James	*Washington Square*
Stephen Crane	*The Red Badge of Courage*
Ralph Waldo Emmerson	*Self-Reliance, & Other Essays (series1&2)*
Sun Tzu	*The Art of War*
Charles Dickens	*A Christmas Carol*
Fyodor Dostoyevsky	*The Gambler; The Double*
Virginia Wolf	*To the Lighthouse; Mrs Dalloway*
Johann W Goethe	*The Sorrows of Young Werther*
Walt Whitman	*Leaves of Grass - 1855 edition*
Confucius	*Analects*
Anonymous	*Beowulf*
Anne Bronte	*Agnes Grey*
More	*Utopia*

full list at: www.azilothbooks.com

Obtainable at all good online and local bookstores.